JAMES B. EADS

The Civil War Ironclads
and
His Mississippi

James B. Eads
(From *A History of the St. Louis Bridge*,
by Calvin Milton Woodward, St. Louis 1881)

JAMES B. EADS

The Civil War Ironclads and His Mississippi

Rex T. Jackson

HERITAGE BOOKS
2007

HERITAGE BOOKS
AN IMPRINT OF HERITAGE BOOKS, INC.

Books, CDs, and more—Worldwide

For our listing of thousands of titles see our website at
www.HeritageBooks.com

Published 2007 by
HERITAGE BOOKS, INC.
Publishing Division
65 East Main Street
Westminster, Maryland 21157-5026

Copyright © 2004 Rex T. Jackson

Other books by the author:
A Trail of Tears: The American Indian in the Civil War
The Sultana Saga: The Titanic of the Mississippi

All rights reserved. No part of this book may be reproduced or transmitted in any form or by any means, electronic or mechanical, including photocopying, recording or by any information storage and retrieval system without written permission from the author, except for the inclusion of brief quotations in a review.

International Standard Book Number: 978-0-7884-2477-7

*Dedicated to my wife
Katherine Marie Jackson,
and also,
to the fourteen unfortunate souls
who lost their lives when the
I-40 bridge near Webber Falls, Oklahoma,
collapsed in 2002.*

Contents

1. Eads' Mississippi   1
2. The Building of "Pook's Turtles"   9
3. An Ironclad War   19
4. Wedding the Nation   31
5. Natural Highway to the Sea   45
6. From Sea to Sea   59
7. Honored Spirits of Bellefontaine Cemetery   65
8. In Great American Company   71
Author's Final Word   77
Acknowledgements   79
Notes   95
Bibliography   105
Chronology   109
Index   113

James B. Eads:
The Civil War Ironclads
and
His Mississippi

Chapter 1

Eads' Mississippi

When pondering the Mississippi River and the role it played in American history, it courses through generations who traveled it, and settled next to its long and winding banks. This untamed mass of flowing water, fed by the run off of America's vast lands, could hardly be conceived to have been mastered by anyone. Yet, there is one person not greatly remembered in the annuls that deserves a closer look. To better appreciate his accomplishments, one need only to stand and face such a mighty river and its awesome power, and scheme to overcome it.

Running north and south slicing through the heart of America is the Mississippi River, named by the Algonguin Indians "Missi-Sipi" (big river), it begins in north-central United States on its long serpentine journey 2,348 miles to the Gulf of Mexico. The Mississippi discharges the largest volume of water of any river in North America - a yearly flow of about 145 cu. mi. of water, with an estimate of about 400,000,000 cu. yd. of sediment carried each year.[1]

In E.W. Gould's book *Fifty Years on the Mississippi*, the word "Mississippi is from the Ojibbeway tongue and signifies, ...great river or rivers of water from all sides."[2] Its ever flowing waters become state boundaries for Minnesota, Iowa, Missouri, Arkansas and Louisiana, on the west side, while Wisconsin, Illinois, Kentucky, Tennessee, and the state of Mississippi, is formed on the east bank. Including its tributaries, there is about 16,090 miles of navigable length in its river-system.[3]

Between 1763 and 1783, the Mississippi separated Great Britain and Spain's control of North America; while after the American Revolution, it served as a boundary for the newly formed United States and the Spanish territory before the Louisiana Purchase. African Americans who were slaves before the Civil War, considered the Mississippi River as a road to freedom "upriver" but to be "sold downriver" an omen of bondage, or slavery.[4]

Early steam vessels to ply the Mississippi were reported to be called "fire canoes" by the Chickasaw Indians.[5] As time went on, the steamboat offered some mastery of the river, which allowed many passengers to travel comfortably to landings up and down the Mississippi and its tributaries. By 1849 a steamboat could travel from New Orleans, Louisiana, to St. Louis, Missouri, in about three to four days. Traveling the rivers by way of these steam powered riverboats had risks as well, and passengers were always relieved to hear the pilot call out "Mark twain" (a safe depth of water). The river had many dangerous obstacles to be aware of - floating logs, debris, ice, sandbars, storms and snags; the fear of an exploding boiler was also an ever present possibility to consider when traveling the river aboard a steamer.[6]

Since the time native Americans first traveled the river by canoe, to the steamboat era and even today, the Mississippi River has played an important role for the nation. Its contribution is a constant flowing current of necessity to our environment and way of life. Throughout history, no person knew, understood, or accomplished more with regard to the Mississippi River, than James Buchanan Eads. His genius as a civil engineer, even though he was unschooled, enabled him to achieve much to overcome the natural powers of the mighty river.

James B. Eads was born in Lawrenceburg, Indiana, on May 23, 1820, and died March 8, 1887. He was named after his mother's cousin, James Buchanan, who became the fifteenth President of the United States of America.[7] In 1884 Eads received the Albert Medal of the Royal Society of the Arts in Great Britain from Queen Victoria; and after his death, he was elected to the Hall of Fame for Great Americans at the New York University in 1920, along with the famous Samuel Clemens and Daniel Boone.[8]

At the age of thirteen, in late summer of 1833, young James Eads moved to St. Louis, Missouri, with his family on board a steamboat, but before reaching their destination the boat burned and sank leaving them without all of their worldly possessions. As a result, James quit school to sell apples on the streets of St. Louis to help provide for his families struggling needs.

For five years James worked as a clerk in a dry good store in St. Louis, where he spent much of his time taking advantage of the owner's private library. After this he took a job as a purser's clerk (mud-clerk), aboard a Mississippi riverboat, the *Knickerbocker*, under Captain Emerson W. Gould, where he became even more familiar with the great river.[9] He also experienced the sinking of the *Knickerbocker*, which went down after being ripped open by a snag. From this, James Eads dared to dream of hunting for sunken treasure submerged within the wrecks that lined the bottom of the Mississippi River.[10] Eads learned that "despite all care that could be used, steamboats were every week sunk and wrecked, and with their valuable engines, boilers, and cargoes were often left where they lay in the ceaseless brown current. After he had been for three years on the river, Eads gave up his clerkship to go into the business of raising these boats, their machinery, and their freight."[11]

At the age of twenty-two James Eads joined with Nelson & Case boat builders and produced the Submarine No. 1. It would be the beginning of a prosperous career, where , according to his grandson Louis How, "his first appearance in the new business was an experience that well shows his quick inventive genius, his persistency, and his courage. While his diving-bell boat was building, a barge loaded with pig-lead sank in the rapids at Keokuk [Iowa], 212 miles from St. Louis. A contract having been made with its owners, Eads hurried up there to rescue the freight from fifteen feet of water. He had no knowledge himself of diving-armor; but he had engaged a skilled diver from the Great Lakes, who brought his own apparatus. They set out in a barge and anchored over the wreck; but, once there, they soon discovered that the current was so exceedingly rapid that the diver could do nothing in it. Eads at once returned to Keokuk, and, buying a forty-gallon whisky hogshead [a large cask], took it out to the wreck; and having knocked out one head, he slung pigs of lead round his improvised diving-bell, made a seat inside it, rigged it to his derrick and air-pumps, and then asked the diver to go down in it. The diver having very naturally refused, Eads on the spot set himself a precedent which, during his after life, he never broke - saying that he would not ask an employee to go where he would not trust himself, he got inside his hogshead and was lowered into the river...Although the rough diving-bell worked awkwardly at first, it served well enough, and finally all of the lost freight was saved."[12]

Eads' river salvage continued, walking the river bottom in his diving bell to guide snag boats to their profitable destinations ahead of other wreckers. In 1848 he built the Submarine No. 2 at Cairo, Illinois, which was "eminently a success."[13]

The Submarine No. 3 came in 1849, and for its first mission, it was called upon to clear the St. Louis harbor of 28 steamboat wrecks that sank there as a result of a great fire at

St. Louis' waterfront. The tragedy took place May 17, 1849, when the riverboat steamer *White Cloud* caught fire destroying many boats, and also spread to fifteen city blocks; and all this while St. Louis was battling a terrible plague of cholera.[14]

The success of the salvage boats was such that "in 1851 the Submarine No. 4 was built at Paducah, Kentucky, and inaugurated a new era in the business of wrecking on Western rivers. She was provided with one of Grimes' patent pumps, which was one of the most powerful ones that had ever been invented, and this company had the sole right to use it on all waters of the Mississippi Valley." It was also said that: "Since 1851, they have raised by the use of this pump some 50 steamboats, a thing before thought to be impossible in many cases."[15]

In the winter of 1856-57, when the St. Louis wharf was lined with steamboats, an early thaw sent large amounts of ice downstream destroying about forty boats in the process. It was Eads to the rescue again, the first steamer he dragged ashore after ten days of hard labor was, the *Garden City*.[16]

Other salvage boats were used, but by 1857, the Submarine No. 7 was built, "and was undoubtedly the most complete boat of [its] kind in the world, and was capable of raising the largest vessels."[17] An even more famous future loomed ahead for No. 7, but as for her first task of salvage, it was said that "she excelled all predecessors and anything that has been constructed since her day."[18] By the time No. 12 arrived, Eads, now thirty-seven years old, was informed by his doctors he needed to retire due to his health.[19]

As time went on, James Eads "grew now to know the river as few have ever known it - his operations extended from Galena, Illinois, to the Balize at the river's very mouth, and even into the tributaries of the Mississippi - and he used to say that there was not a stretch of fifty miles in the twelve hundred between St. Louis and New Orleans in which he had not stood on the bottom under his diving-bell."[20]

Eads' experiences at the bottom of the Mississippi were

many. On one occasion he tells about a time a few miles below Cairo, Illinois: "...I searched the river bottom for the wreck of the Neptune, for more than sixty days, and in a distance of three miles. My boat was held by a long anchor line, and was swung from side to side of the channel, over a distance of 500 feet, by side anchor lines, while I walked on the river bottom under the bell across the channel. The boat was then dropped twenty feet farther down stream, and I then walked back again as she was hauled toward the other shore. In this way I walked on the bottom four hours at least, every day (Sundays excepted) during that time."[21]

With the issue of slavery, secession, and state's rights becoming a hotbed of controversy, it seemed that war loomed upon the horizon. On April 12, 1861, shots at Fort Sumter brought that reality into the light of day. James Eads, believing that the Union would need to control the Mississippi River, supported the idea of an inland river navy. He insisted that armored gunboats be built and used against Confederate boats, fortifications, and shore batteries, that were already being constructed and put into place.

James Eads' calling to the Mississippi River was not to end with the fortune he had made under his diving bell. His ingenuity, and inventive engineering genius of his generation, would not allow him to go unnoticed by a nation thrown into war and in crisis. His river had gained a firm hold upon his soul, and not even the tuberculosis and effects of decompression, due to the many trips he had made to the bottom of it,[22] would detour his resolve. A determined Eads would also answer the call of his country, and the powerful creation of his expertise would become the instruments of victory - he would be asked to claim his river and her tributaries for the Union in the Civil War.

On April 17, 1861, not long after the Confederacy had taken command of Fort Sumter at Charleston, North Carolina, James Eads received a letter from Attorney-General Bates which conveyed Washington's confidence in him, saying: "Be not surprised if you are called here suddenly by telegram. If called, come instantly. In a certain contingency it will be necessary to have the aid of the most thorough knowledge of our Western rivers and the use of steam on them, and in that event I have advised that you should be consulted."[23]

The President called a cabinet meeting to consider Eads' proposals and recommendations. His plan was to set into motion an inland navy that would spearhead an amphibious drive to reclaim the Lower Mississippi from the Confederacy.[24]

In a rush to create a fleet of powerful armored riverboats, "bids were opened on the 5th of August, 1861, and Mr. Eads was found to be the best bidder for the whole number, both in regard to the time of completion and price...On the 7th of August, 1861, Mr. Eads signed a contract with Quartermaster-General Meigs to construct these seven vessels ready for their crews and armaments in sixty-five days."[25]

The contract stipulated that the iron-plated boats were to be delivered on the 10th of October, 1861, at Cairo, Illinois. The boats, however, were not sent until late November with a considerable amount of work yet to be done. It wasn't until January 15, 1862, that they were finally complete and accepted. Lack of payment and alterations in design had caused the delay of the original date of delivery.[26]

Eads knew how much the Union needed the gunboats, and made the statement that it was "of the utmost importance that these boats should be made as effective as possible, without reference to how I was to be affected by delays, ...and that their completion should be pushed with the utmost energy, whether the government failed in its part of the bargain or not."[27]

The needs of the Union had found a home in the "ability to get things done" persona, of Captain James B. Eads. By "the rapid completion of so many gunboats for the government at the breaking out of the war was alone sufficient to give him a national reputation as one of the master minds in its service, and second to none in mechanical ingenuity, and superior to all in perseverance."[28]

Even though his creation of the ironclads was not the first war steamer, they would nevertheless prove worthy of everything that Eads had envisioned them to be for the purpose they were designed for - an innovation for their time. His iron plated war machines would enable the Union to reclaim his Mississippi and split the Confederacy in two.

Chapter 2

The Building of "Pook's Turtles"

A few decades before Eads would answer the call of constructing his steam powered ironclads, which according to Alfred T. Mahan in his book *The Gulf and Inland Waters*, bore "no small resemblance to gigantic turtles wallowing slowly along in their native element,"[1] Robert Fulton, would propose to build a steam propelled warship (or floating battery) to the President of the United States. Called the *Demologus*, Fulton was appointed the engineer, and on June 20, 1814, at the Adam and Noah shipyard in New York City, New York, the keels were laid.[2]

On October 20, 1814, while scores looked on, the *Demologus*, or afterward named the *Fulton*, was launched. The dimensions of the *Fulton the First* were: "Length, 150 feet, breadth, 56 feet, depth, 20 feet, water-wheel, 16 feet diameter, length of bucket, 14 feet, dip, 4 feet, engine, 48 inch cylinder, 5 feet stroke; boiler 22 feet length, breadth 12 feet, and depth 8 feet. Tonnage 2, 475. She was the largest steamer by many hundreds of tons that had been built at the date of her launch."[3]

A letter written by Captain David Porter to the Secretary of the Navy stated, that: "I have the pleasure to inform you that the *Fulton the First*, was this morning safely launched. No one yet has ventured to suggest any improvement that could be made in the vessel...She promises fair to answer our most sanguine expectations, and I do not despair in being able to navigate in her from one extreme end of the coast to the other. Her buoyancy astonishes every one. She now draws only eight feet three inches of water, and her draft will be ten feet when her guns, machinery stores and crew are all on board."[4]

A report made by the commissioner, after a thorough examination of the *Fulton the First*, said that: "She is a structure resting on two boats, keels separated from end to end by a canal 15 feet wide and 60 feet long. One boat contains the cauldrons of copper to prepare her steam. The vast cylinder of iron with its pistons, levers and wheels occupies a part of its fellow. The great water-wheel revolves in the space between them. The main or gun deck, supporting her armament is protected by a bulwark four feet ten inches thick, of solid timber. This is pierced by thirty port holes to enable as many as thirty-two pounders to fire red hot balls. Her upper or spar deck, upon which several thousand men might parade, is encompassed by a bulwark which affords safe quarters. She is rigged by two short masts, each of which supports a large lateen yawl and sails. She has two bowsprits and gibs and four rudders, two at each extremity of the boat so that she can be steered either end foremost. Her machinery is calculated for the addition of an engine which will discharge an immense column of hot water, which is intended to throw upon the decks and all through the ports of an enemy. If in addition to all of this we suppose her to be finished according to Mr. Fulton's intention, with one hundred pounder

Columbiads, two suspended from each bow, so as to discharge a ball of that size into an enemy's ship, ten or twelve feet below the water line, it must be allowed that she has the appearance at least of being the most formidable engine of warfare that human ingenuity has contrived."[5]

As for the iron plated gunboats of Eads' inland navy fleet, their design resembling large turtles, would be needed for the War Between the States. These iron shelled river warcraft were to be built after the designs of Samuel M. Pook, and because of their prominent feature, become known as "Pook's Turtles."[6]

Just south of St. Louis, Missouri, was the Carondelet shipyard, first established by a man named Primus Emerson and called the Carondelet Marine Railway Company, was leased to James Eads where he would build, with the help of about four thousand men working night and day seven days a week, four city-class gunboats: the *Carondelet, St. Louis, Louisville,* and the *Pittsburgh*; but soon after, the old war horse *Benton* would also be built which was converted from the *Submarine No. 7*. The *Mound City, Cincinnati* and *Cairo,* were to be built across the Mississippi River at Mound City, Illinois.[7]

A month after Eads' ironclads had already been used successfully to capture Fort Henry, "a victory exclusively for the gunboats,"[8] the famous battle of the *Monitor* and the *Merrimac* occurred, on March 9, 1862, at Hampton Roads, Virginia. The wooden hulled *Merrimac* layered with two-inch-thick iron plating and armed with ten guns, engaged the smaller but more radical designed *Monitor* ironclad with its armament and revolving turret equipped with two eleven-inch guns. The battle raged on for two hours, as the historic duel fired thunderous shell after shell at each other but without either of them scoring a fatal blow, the clash ended as a draw.[9]

It was said of the engagement between the *Merrimac* (or the *Virginia* as it was known by the South), and the *Monitor,* that it was "in some respects the most momentous naval conflict ever witnessed. No battle was ever more widely discussed or produced a greater sensation. It revolutionized the navies of the world...Rams and iron-clads were in future to decide all naval warfare. In this battle old things passed away, and the experience of a thousand years of battle and breeze was forgotten."[10]

In a private letter, written by Lieutenant S. Dana Greene executive officer of the *Monitor* shortly after the battle, he wrote: "My men and myself were perfectly black with smoke and powder. All my underclothes were perfectly black, and my person was in the same condition...I had been up so long, and been under such a state of excitement, that my nervous system was completely run down...My nerves and muscles twitched as though electric shocks were continually passing through them...I lay down and tried to sleep - I might as well have tried to fly."[11]

Lieutenant Greene's faith in the *Monitor* was such that he felt it necessary to write some years later, that: "No ship in the world's history has a more imperishable place in naval annuls than the *Monitor*. Not only by her providential arrival at the right moment did she secure the safety of Hampton Roads and all that depended on it, but the idea which she embodied revolutionized the system of naval warfare which had existed from the earliest recorded history..."[12]

The powerful river ironclad turtles designed by Samuel Pook and built by James Eads, would do much to gain control of the Mississippi and its tributaries for the Union, but would also be destined to be remembered in the shadows of the sea vessels *Merrimac* and *Monitor*; even though Eads' inland boats were first to fight successfully. James Eads would protect his beloved Mississippi.

The *DeKalb* (called the *St. Louis* at first), *Carondelet*, *Cincinnati*, *Louisville*, *Mound City*, *Cairo*, and *Pittsburgh*, were "one hundred and seventy-five feet long and fifty feet beam. The propelling power was one large paddle-wheel, which was placed in an opening prepared for it, midway of the breadth of the vessel and a little forward of the stern, in such wise as to be materially protected by the sides and casemate [armored enclosure]. This opening, which was eighteen feet wide, extended forward sixty feet from the stern, dividing the after-body into two parts, which were connected abaft the wheel by planking thrown from one side to the other. This after-part was called the fantail. The casemate extended from the curve of the bow to that of the stern, and was carried across the deck both forward and aft, thus forming a square box, whose sides sloped in and up at an angle of forty-five degrees, containing the battery, the machinery, and the paddle-wheel. The casemate was pierced for thirteen guns, three in the forward end ranging directly ahead, four on each broadside, and two stern guns."[13]

As the riverine vessels were expected to fight bow to bow in most cases, the front bow section casemate was made of iron armor two and a half inches thick, backed by twenty-four inches of oak hardwood.[14] Much of the iron came by way of Pittsburgh, Pennsylvania, and reportedly, some of the iron plate came from the Maramec Iron Works of Maramec Springs, Missouri.[15] While beneath the plating of the gun deck casemate was twenty inches of timber, with "its grain running up from the water instead of horizontally, by which means [wrote Eads] a ball will strike, as it were, with the grain, and then be more readily deflected. On the same principle that a mini ball will penetrate five inches of oak, crossing the grain, while it will not enter one inch if fired at the end [end grain] of the timber." This detail illustrates the careful thought that Eads put into the construction of the boats.[16]

The vessels were armed with four old 42-pounders, which were rifled, and fired a 70-pound shell, six 32-pounders, and three 8-inch guns.[17] The Merritt engines propelled the steamers at a speed of 9 miles per hour, by way of 22-inch cast iron cylinders with strokes of 6 feet.[18]

Soon after the creation of the first seven gunboats, the twin hulled snag boat *Submarine No. 7*, which had been "purchased by, not built for, the Government," was converted by Eads into the *Benton*, the most formidable ironclad ever built - a great flagship for the Union's inland navy flotillas. The giant *Benton* was built much the same as the other seven boats, but much larger. "Her size was 1,000 tons, double that of the seven; length 202 feet; extreme breadth 72 feet. The forward plating was 3 inches of iron, backed by 30 inches of oak; at the stern, and abreast the engines, there was 2 ½ inch iron, backed by 12 inches of oak; the rest of the sides of the casemates was covered with five-eights inch iron."[19] Eads reported that: "She was built with two hulls about twenty feet apart, very strongly braced together. She had been purchased by General Fremont while he was in command of the Western Department, and had been sent to my ship-yard for alteration into a gun-boat. I had the space between the two hulls planked, so that a continuous bottom extended from the other side of one hull to the other side of the other. The upper side was decked over in the same manner; and by extending the outer sides of the two hulls forward until they joined each other at a new stem, which received them, the twin boats became one wide, strong, and substantial hull. The new bottom did not extend to the stern of the hull, but was brought up to the deck fifty feet forward of the stern, so as to have a space for a central wheel with which the boat was to be propelled. This wheel was turned by the original engines of the snag-boat, each of the engines having formerly turned an independent wheel on the outside of the twin boat. In this manner the *Benton* became a war vessel of about seventy-five feet beam, a greater breadth, perhaps, than that of any war vessel then afloat."[20] He went on to say, that: "A slanting casemate, covered with iron plates, was placed over her sides and across her bow and stern; and the wheel was protected in a similar manner. The casemate on the sides and bow was covered with iron 3 ½ inches thick; the wheel-house and stern with lighter plates, like the first seven boats built by me."[21] Out of the 16 gun armament, were two 9-inch shell guns, seven rifled army 42-pounders, and seven 32-pounders. With all of the guns and stores on board, the *Benton* drew nine feet of water, with a speed of only five knots an hour. Flag Officer Foote, writing to Quartermaster General Meigs, had this to say about the leviathan: "The *Benton* is greatly superior to any gunboat I have ever seen. Every officer here pronounces her the best gunboat in the Union."[22] The *Benton*, with the other seven, "may be fairly called the ships of the line of battle on western waters."[23]

In the spring of 1862 James Eads was again called to Washington, this time to be asked to build two lighter ironclad river monitors, the *Osage* and the *Neosho*, with rotating turrets. Being very anxious for the chance to construct the boats with turrets, he explains: "I was very anxious to construct these turrets after a plan which I had devised, quite different from the Ericsson or Coles system, and in which the guns should be operated by steam. But, within a month after the engagement at Fort Donelson, the memorable contest between the *Merrimac* and the *Monitor* occurred, whereupon the Navy Department insisted on Ericsson turrets being placed upon these two vessels."[24]

He was also contracted at this time to build four larger ironclad monitors with two turrets on each, the *Chickasaw*, *Milwaukee*, *Winnebago*, and the *Kickapoo*, and was allowed, at his own risk, to equip the *Chickasaw* and the *Milwaukee* with one of his steam powered turrets on each; which would have been replaced by the John Ericsson turret at his own cost had they failed. Eads' steam turret was the first turret to manipulate heavy artillery by the use of steam power, and they could fire an impressive every forty-five seconds, which was seven times faster than the Ericsson turret.[25] According to Navy inspector J.W. King in a report to the Navy Department, he spoke about Eads' turret, saying that: "The design, construction and arrangement of the details of the machinery is highly creditable to the ingenuity, mechanical skill and ability of the inventor...who had to contend with the disadvantages common to a light draft vessel."[26]

The men that were recruited for Eads' ironclads were taken from various sources - army soldiers, volunteers who had previous experience aboard riverboats, pilots and engineers, as well as salt water sailors known as Jack Tars.[27] Life aboard these riverine iron war turtles was not for the claustrophobic or faint of heart, Henry Walke, Rear Admiral, N.S.N., of the *Carondelet*, shares one of his amazing war stories: "We heard the deafening crack of the bursting shells, the crash of the solid shot, and the whizzing of fragments of shells and wood as they sped through the vessel. Soon a 128-pounder struck our anchor, smashed it into flying bolts, and bounded over the vessel, taking away a part of our smoke-stack; then another cut away the iron boat-davits as if they were pipe-stems, whereupon the boat dropped into the water. Another ripped the iron plating and glanced over; another went through the plating and lodged in the heavy casemate; another struck the pilot-house, knocked the plating to pieces, and sent fragments of iron and splinters into pilots, one of whom fell mortally wounded, and was taken below; another shot took away the remaining boat-davits and the boat with them; and still they came, harder and faster, taking flag-staffs and smoke-stacks, and tearing off the side armor as lightning tears the bark from a tree. Our men fought desperately, but, under the excitement of the occasion, loaded too hastily, and the port rifled gun exploded. One of the crew, in his account of the explosion soon after it occurred, said: 'I was serving the gun with shell. When it exploded it knocked us all down, killing none, but wounding over a dozen men and spreading dismay and confusion among us. For about two minutes I was stunned, and at least five minutes elapsed before I could tell what was the matter. When I found out that I was more scared than hurt, although suffering from the gunpowder which I had inhaled, I looked forward and saw our gun lying on the deck, split in three pieces. Then the cry ran through the boat that we were on fire, and my duty as a pump-man called me to the pumps. While I was there, two shots entered our bow-ports and killed four men and wounded several others. They were borne past me, three with their heads off. The sight almost sickened me, and I turned my head away.' "[28]

With about 250 inland navy men cramped aboard one of these Civil War ironclads, it would be hard enough to imagine what it must have been like on a daily basis, let alone, in the din and blue-gray smoke of a fierce broadside conflict blazing gun to gun on a river battleground. The journey ahead for "Pook's Turtles," would take them and their brave crews to many such river fields of battle, where slow and steady would eventually win the race for the Union and the dedicated James Eads.

Chapter 3

An Ironclad War

With their crews, armament and stores on board, Eads' fleet of ironclads took to the water adorned for war. Before them, lay the challenge for which they were so hurriedly and hastily produced. By this time, along the shorelines of the Mississippi and its tributaries, were hostile foes that separated James Eads from his passion of engineering further river development for the betterment of the nation. With his future projects disrupted by Civil War, his gunboats would have to make war. As the river, and all who perchance witnessed these strange new iron creatures watched in amazement, the flotilla moved slowly down the Mississippi ready on command to spew out a lethal combination of their deadly and angry projectiles - heavy shot and shell.

By February 1861, Flag Officer Foote, in command of the Western flotilla, were approaching Fort Henry on the Tennessee River fishing up dangerous Confederate torpedoes (mines) out of the river as they went along. The torpedoes were described as consisting "of a stout sheet-iron cylinder, pointed at both ends, about 5½ feet long and 1 foot in diameter. The iron lever was 3½ feet long, and armed with prongs to catch the bottom of the boat. This lever was constructed to move the iron rod on the inside of the cylinder, thus acting as a trigger of the lock to explode the cap and fire the powder. The machine was anchored, presenting the prongs in such a way that boats going down-stream should slide over them, but those coming up should catch."[1] It was fortunate for Foote's fleet that the flood stage of the river had disabled many of the devices by washing them away.[2]

These Confederate-type torpedoes also found their way to be used as a weapon fitted to the end of a long pole, which was used by the famous CSS *H.L. Hunley* to sink the USS *Housatonic* on February 17, 1864, off the coast of Charleston, North Carolina. The *H.L. Hunley* was the world's first ever combat submarine, cigar-shaped and made of iron, it sank three times and gained a ghastly reputation of taking brave lives into eternity, including its own inventor, Horace Lawson Hunley. About the *Hunley*, First Engineer James H. Tomb of the C. S. Navy, speaking about it and its final mission, said that his "understanding was that from the time of her construction at Mobile [Alabama] up to the time when she struck *Housatonic* not less than 33 men had lost their lives in her. She was a veritable coffin to this brave officer and his men."[3]

The *Hunley* was designed for about an eight man crew to propel, at a top speed of 3 knots, by the use of a hand crank that ran the length of the 30 feet long, by 5 feet high and 4 feet wide, submersible craft. Its mission was to ram and stick a torpedo into the wooden hulls of unsuspecting Union ships, then, back away to safety; but after successfully delivering the device that sank the *Housatonic*, it sank under mysterious circumstances shortly after, and for the last time took its crew to a watery grave and the afterlife.

On February 6, 1862, Flag Officer Foote, in the temporary

flagship *Cincinnati,* commanded by R.N. Stemble, were ready to move against Fort Henry, along with the *Carondelet,* under Commander H. Walke, the *St. Louis,* under Lieutenant Commander L. Spaulding, the *Essex,* under Commander W.D. Porter, and the three timberclads, the *Tyler,* under Lieutenant Commander William Gwin, the *Lexington,* under Lieutenant Commander J.W. Shirk, and finally, the *Conestoga,* commanded by Lieutenant Commander S.L. Phelps.[4]

Fort Henry was a fortification that lay on the east bank of the Tennessee River. Constructed in a marshy low lying area, it was always susceptible to flood waters; but it also made it less vulnerable to attack by ground forces. For its defense, the fort was protected by six 32-pounders, two 42-pounders, five 18-pounders, one 6-inch rifled gun, and one large 128-pounder Columbaid.[5]

The flotilla crept slowly toward the fort in the quiet of the scenic wooded surroundings that lined the Tennessee shore. The crews of the fleet stood at their posts anticipating a possible victory or defeat only moments away. Around noon, as the peaceful morning they had been basking in gave way to an uncertain afternoon, a bold and defiant flag of the Confederacy above Fort Henry came into view. Their powerful guns were well manned and protected by newly formed earth works, all of which would soon come to bear on the flotilla - every man waxed ready.

As the flag steamer *Cincinnati* came within firing range of the fort, the order was given to fire the first shot, signaling the rest of the fleet to follow suit. An intense battle ensued as the Confederates retaliated. "At once the fort was ablaze with the flame of her eleven heavy guns. The wild whistle of their rifle-shells was heard on every side..."[6]

According to Commander Walke, the response from the riverboats was no less impressive. "The firing from the armored vessels was rapid and well sustained from the beginning of the attack, and seemingly accurate, as we could occasionally see the earth thrown in great heaps over the enemy's guns." The commander of the *Carondelet* went on to say that the fire from the fort was not to be despised, "their heavy shot broke and scattered our iron-plating as if it had been putty, and often passed completely through the casemates. But our old men-of-war's men, captains of the guns, proud to show their worth in battle, infused life and courage into their young comrades. When these experienced gunners saw a shot coming toward a port, they had the coolness and discretion to order their men to bow down, to save their heads."[7]

The Confederate gunners, having practiced before the riverine fleet arrived with range and distance, were deadly accurate against the gunboats. With one boat it was like "a thunder-bolt, ripping her side-timbers and scattering the splinters over the vessel."[8] The ironclads, on the other hand, with their protective casemates and formidable armament, soon brought silence to Fort Henry. After about two hours of heavy artillery, in a cloud of sulfurous smoke, Confederate General Tilghman lowered his flag; but not before he had sent about 2,600 men to the safety of nearby Fort Donelson. Defeated Fort Henry was secured for the arrival of General Grant and his men who, "had expected his troops to take part in a land attack, but the heavy rains had made the direct roads to the fort almost impassable."[9]

When surrendering to Flag Officer Foote, it was reported that General Tilghman said that he was "glad to surrender to so gallant an officer," to which Foote reportedly replied, "You do perfectly right, sir, in surrendering, but you should have blown my boat out of the water before I would have surrendered to you." Commander Walke later wrote, that: "I was with Foote soon after the surrender, and I cannot believe that such a reply was made by him. He was too much a gentleman to say anything calculated to wound the feelings of an officer who had defended his post with signal courage and fidelity, and whose spirits were clouded by the adverse fortunes of war."[10]

The cheers of victory and surrender quickly faded out of sight after the striking of the Confederate colors, for inside the fort the sight was sobering. "On every side the blood of the dead and wounded was intermingled with the earth and their implements of war."[11] Never before had hostile land forces surrendered solely to the Navy, which would not happen again throughout the Civil War.[12]

With Eads' boats still unpaid for by this time, nevertheless, the Federal government wasted no time in their employment. Not long after the battle of Fort Henry, the gunboats were already steaming under power towards a next, more difficult assignment.

On a commanding bluff 120 feet high on the west bank overlooking the Cumberland River, set a Confederate held stronghold - Fort Donelson. The fortification had artillery batteries in three strategic locations. Its 15 guns were dispersed in these, at about twenty-feet above the river, about fifty-feet, and atop the bluff; all in all, a very good defensive position.[13]

On a balmy February 13, 1862, Commander Walke of the *Carondelet*, by request of General Grant, was in place near Fort Donelson awaiting further orders. He then received a dispatch from General Grant informing him that his army was in position "almost entirely investing the enemy's works." In the dispatch Grant told Walke, that: "Most of our batteries are established, and the remainder soon will be. If you will advance with your gun-boat at 10 o'clock in the morning, we will be ready to take advantage of any diversion in our favor."[14] Grant would have about 15,000 men and eight batteries, with more fresh reinforcements expected to join-up soon.[15]

At 9:05 on the morning of February 14, 1862, the *Carondelet* would heave 139 70-pound and 64-pound shells toward Fort Donelson. In response, the fort fired its guns at the *Carondelet* with only two shots causing damage. One of these balls, a 128-pound solid shot, was described by Henry Walke in his article *The Western Flotilla at Fort Donelson, Island Number Ten, Fort Pillow and Memphis*, as having "struck the corner of our port broadside casemate, passed through it, and in its progress toward the center of our boilers glanced over the temporary barricade in front of the boilers. It then passed over the steam-drum, struck the beams of the upper deck, carried away the railing around the engine-room and burst the steam-heater, and, glancing back into the engine-room, 'seemed to bound after the men,' as one of the engineers said, 'like a wild beast pursuing its prey.' I have preserved this ball as a souvenir of the fight at Fort Donelson." Walke went on to say that: "When it burst through the side of the *Carondelet*, it knocked down and wounded a dozen men, seven of them severely. An immense quantity of splinters was blown through the vessel. Some of them, as fine as needles, shot through the clothes of the men like arrows. Several of the wounded were so much excited by the suddenness of the event and the sufferings of their comrades, that they were not aware that they themselves had been struck until they felt the blood running into their shoes. Upon receiving this shot we ceased firing for a while." [16]

At about 3 o'clock in the afternoon the flotilla advanced toward the fort, the *Louisville* on the west side of the river, the *St. Louis*, serving as the flag-steamer, and the *Ptttsburgh* and the *Carondelet* on the east side. The timberclads took up the rear.[17] The close proximity of the gunboats to the fort allowed the Confederates to pound the smokestacks, pepper the armored casemates, and penetrate decks and pilot houses into the boats innermost bowls; while the Union flotilla overshot their intended targets.[18] The fleet suffered severe blows as a result.

The reality of the battle at Fort Donelson aboard one of Eads' ironclads was graphically described by the Commander of the *Carondelet*: "Our gunners kept up a constant firing while we were falling back; and the warning words, 'Look out!' 'Down!' were often heard, and heeded by nearly all the gun-crews. On one occasion, while the men were at the muzzle of the middle bow-gun, loading it, the warning came just in time for them to jump aside as a 32-pounder struck the lower sill, and glancing up struck the upper sill, bounded on deck and spun around like a top, but hurt no one. It was very evident that if the men who were loading had not obeyed the order to drop, several of them would have been killed. So I repeated the instructions and warned the men at the guns and the crew generally to bow or stand off from the ports when a shot was seen coming. But some of the young men, from a spirit of bravado or from a belief in the doctrine of fatalism, disregarded the instructions, saying it was useless to attempt to dodge a cannonball, and they would trust to luck. The warning words, 'Look out!' 'Down!' were again heard; down went the gunner and his men, as the whizzing shot glanced on the gun, taking off the gunner's cap and the heads of two of the young men who trusted to luck, and in defiance of the order were standing up or passing behind him. This shot killed another man also, who was at the last gun of the starboard side, and disabled the gun. It came in with a hissing sound; three sharp spats and a heavy bang told the sad fate of three brave comrades. Before the decks were well sanded, there was so much blood on them that our men could not work the guns without slipping."[19]

The air that had been charged with flying missiles that day, had left Fort Donelson and her brave Confederates with a victorious feeling. In Flag Officer Foote's report of the day's events, he said: "The officers and men in this hotly contested but unequal fight behaved with the greatest gallantry and determination."[20]

After the unseasonable warm weather they had been experiencing that day, the night of the 14th became bitter cold. The wind howled a terrible song while thousands tried to sleep in the great outdoors, in ditches, or anywhere that afforded some escape from the driving, freezing, unforgiving rain and snow.[21] The elements became the enemy that night.

Day brought with it, not just the frigid winter like weather, but a renewed engagement between these rivals for the prize of Fort Donelson and the Cumberland River. The 15th also brought with it a time to bury fallen comrades where, "sailors bore their late companions to a lonely field within the shadows of the hills. When they were about to lower the first coffin, a Roman Catholic priest appeared, and his services being accepted, he read the prayers for the dead. As the last services was ended, the sound of the battle being waged by General Grant, like the rumbling of distant thunder, was the only requiem [dirge] for our departed shipmates."[22] On February 16, 1862, Fort Donelson surrendered to the Union. The fleet would lick their wounds in preparation for further orders; the *Carondelet* and *Pittsburgh* would return to Cairo, Illinois, for repairs; while the rest of the fleet would hold over at nearby Dover, Tennessee.

After the fall of Columbus, Kentucky, the Confederates, under General Pierre G.T. Beauregard, chose to fall back upon Island Number 10, an island in a series of islands that lay below Cairo on the Mississippi River. The island would become a Confederate military stronghold, about "two miles long by one-third that distance wide, and its general direction was nearly east and west."[23] New Madrid, Missouri, on the west side of the Mississippi, was on a bend where the river ran more west and south. After the evacuation of Columbus, southern forces fortified New Madrid and deployed batteries on Island No. 10 and the Tennessee eastern shoreline above it. "On the island itself were four batteries mounting twenty-three guns, on the Tennessee shore six batteries mounting thirty-two guns. There was also a floating battery, which at the beginning of the operations, was moored abreast the middle of the island, and [was] variously reported as carrying nine or ten 9-inch guns."[24] On February 28, 1862, Brigadier General John Pope, commanding the Union Army of the Mississippi, left Commerce, Missouri, marching through swamps lugging heavy supplies and equipment, and reached New Madrid on the 3rd of March, where it was kept under siege until the 13th. After a heavy Federal bombardment, the Confederate troops and gunboats abandoned New Madrid and retreated to Island No. 10. On the following day, March 14, 1862, Brigadier General Pope's army marched unopposed into the town of New Madrid. The very next day, Commander Flag

Officer Foote and his flotilla arrived in the area. "There were six ironclads, one of which was the *Benton* carrying the flag-officer's flag, and ten mortar-boats."[25] A bombardment of the Tennessee shore and the island was made "throughout the month."[26]

The fortified position of Island No. 10 on the Mississippi, became an important military objective for the Union. General Pope, who had an army of about 20,000 men, was below the island and intended to cross the river and make an assault from below; but needed the help of a gunboat below the island to provide cover fire to silence enemy batteries, so that his troops could cross the river safely. He wrote several times to Flag Officer Foote, and in one of his letters of appeal said "that a boat could pass down at night under cover of darkness."[27] Foote's reply to this was that an attempt "would result in the sacrifice of the boat, her officers and men, which sacrifice I would not be justified to make."[28] It would in the near future become, "not only one of the most daring and dramatic events of the war; it was also the death-blow to the Confederate defense of this position."[29]

After a couple of meetings between Flag Officer Foote and his commanders the idea was rejected, but the brave persistence of Commander Henry Walke of the *Carondelet*, finally won out - he would run the gauntlet of nearly fifty hungry Confederate guns. It would become a memorable undertaking.

Commander Walke tells his story of that historic eventful night, saying: "Having received written orders from the flag-officer, under date of March 30th, I at once began to prepare the *Carondelet* for the ordeal. All the loose material at hand was collected, and on the 4th of April the decks were covered with it, to protect them against plunging shot. Hawsers and chain cables were placed around the pilot-house and other vulnerable parts of the vessel, and every precaution was adopted to prevent disaster. A coal-barge laden with hay and coal was lashed to the part of the port side on which there was no iron plating, to protect the magazine. It was truly said that the *Carondelet* at that time resembled a farmer's wagon prepared for market. The engineers led the escape-steam, through the pipes aft, into the wheel-house, to avoid the puffing sound it made when blown through the smoke-stacks.

"All the necessary preparations having been made, I informed the flag-officer of my intention to run the gauntlet that night, and received his approval...At 10 o'clock the moon had gone down, and the sky, the earth, and the river were alike hidden in the black shadow of a thunder-storm, which had now spread itself over all the heavens. As the time seemed favorable, I ordered the first master to cast off. Dark clouds now rose rapidly over us and enveloped us in almost total darkness, except when the sky was lighted up by the welcome flashes of vivid lightning, to show us the perilous way we were to take...With such vivid lightning as prevailed during the whole passage, there was no prospect of escaping the vigilance of the enemy, but there was good reason to hope that he would be unable to point his guns accurately." After being spotted by Batteries Nos. 2, 3, and 4, they roared into action, and from the "mainland came the continued crack and scream of their rifle-shells, which seemed to unite with the electric batteries of the clouds to annihilate us.

"Having passed the principle batteries, we were greatly relieved from suspense, patiently endured, however, by the officers and crew. But there was another formidable obstacle in the way - a floating battery, which was the great 'war elephant' of the Confederates, built to blockade the Mississippi permanently. As we passed her she fired six or eight shots at us, but without effect...We arrived at New Madrid about midnight with no one hurt, and were most joyfully received by our army."[30]

Not long afterward, the *Pittsburgh* also passed into history and Island No. 10 eventually surrendered to Flag Officer Foote. The *Carondelet* had become known as the gunboat that "struck the blow that secured that victory." It was April 7, 1862, the same day that the Confederates were repulsed at the battle of Shiloh.[31]

The operations would continue for the fleet, and in the campaign for Vicksburg, Mississippi, the objective being "to establish communication from Ohio to the Gulf, and to cut off the important supplies drawn by the Confederacy from Arkansas, Louisiana, and Texas."[32]

On the morning of June 17, 1862, on the White River in the neighborhood of St. Charles, Arkansas, about ninety miles from the river's mouth, the *Mound City, St. Louis, Lexington* and *Conestoga* were engaged by Major-General Thomas C. Hindman's Confederates. From the trees and bushes on the bluffs above the White River the flotilla received fire from Lieutenant Joseph Fry and Lieutenant Dunnington's Confederate guns.

About 600 yards from the hostile batteries, the *Mound City*, who had lead the way into the attack, was hit in its port casemate by a 32-pounder rifle shot. Commander Colonel Graham N. Fitch of the fleet, later described it in his report as "the larboard forequarter of the gunboat."[33] The shot killed 8 men and struck the steam-drum fore and aft, which, "upon the explosion of the steam-drum, was beyond description. The gun-deck was at once filled with scalding steam, and many of the crew were instantly killed, - literally cooked alive. Others, in an agony of pain, jumped into the water, where they were shot at by sharpshooters from the bluff...The boats from the other vessels put off at once to the rescue, and were riddled with shot while picking up their comrades. Out of 175 officers and men on board the *Mound City*, only 23 answered to their names at the roll-call that evening, and these were men and boys that were in the shell-room and magazine when the explosion took place."[34]

The Civil War raged on until the spring of 1865; through it all, it was the work of James Eads and his fleet of gunboats, in conjunction with the Union army, that opened the Mississippi as a superhighway to an inevitable overall victory. As with the success of his diving bell and wrecking company, to the Yankee ingenuity of the Civil War Ironclads, his passion for challenge was far from over - he would have to wed the east and the west and do the impossible, by spanning his wide Mississippi.

Chapter 4

Wedding the Nation

American author Mark Twain of Hannibal, Missouri, wrote of his life growing up along its mighty river. He described it as "the great Mississippi, rolling its mile-wide tide along, shining in the sun; the dense forest away on the other side; the 'point' above the town, and the 'point' below, bounding the river-glimpse and turning it into a sort of sea, and withal a very still and brilliant and lonely one."[1] From his home in that small hamlet overlooking the vast, wide Mississippi, he could envision now famous classic tales in which the river was their backbone. Life on the Mississippi would instill also, inspiration and greatness within more than an aspiring Twain; as with James B. Eads, who knew the Mississippi like no other, his life on its banks would continue to bring out his genius as well. His story would be set, not at Hannibal but at St. Louis, where he would envision a grand steel arched bridge that would, when constructed, become the first roadway to span the Mississippi River and unite the nation together as one.

The construction of a bridge over such waters as vast as the Mississippi could leave almost anyone in awe and respect of its power, Charles Ellet, who had proposed a possible bridge over it himself, said that: "The power of this great river does not prohibit any attempt to restrain, to force, or to change its current; on the contrary, it may be wholly subject to the control of art. Apparently, it varies its depth, alters its direction, reduces or increases its width, with regard only to its boundless power; but these movements are all made in obedience to certain laws, uniform and universal in their action, to the rule of which it is as completely subject as any other effect in nature to the cause by which it is produced. To govern it, the labor of man must be applied with a knowledge of the influences which it recognizes; and that power which renders it apparently so difficult to restrain may then be made the means of its subjection."[2]

Calvin Milton Woodward, who authored *A History of the St. Louis Bridge*, felt that: "There is something almost sublime in the immense volume and apparently irresistible power of this great river. The ease with which it devours island after island, and forms for itself a new channel; the wild deluge of waters with which, without apparent loss of size, it covers thousands of miles of fertile fields; and the unequalled strength and depth of its current, - suggest a power so far beyond human control as to seem almost lawless; and yet nothing is more certain than that, in all its moods and phases, it is wholly obedient to nature's laws, and that the engineer who would grapple with the problems involved in the practical management of the Mississippi, must study and master those inflexible ordinances."[3]

Similar sentiments were shared by James Eads in his study of the river, to which he had this to say: "My experience of this current has taught me that eternal vigilance is the price of safety, and constant watchfulness is one of the first requisites to insure success, almost as much as knowledge and experience. To the superficial observer, this stream seems to override old established theories, and to set at naught the apparently best-devised schemes of science. But yet there moves no grain of sand through its devious channel, in its course to the sea, that is not governed by laws more fixed than any that were known to the code of the Medes and Persians. No giant tree, standing on its banks, bows its stately head beneath these dark waters, except in obedience to laws which have been created, in the goodness and wisdom of Our Heavenly Father, to govern the conditions of matter at rest and in motion."[4]

The craft of bridge building was not without danger or failure, throughout history, many lives were lost and accomplishments dashed by ill-fated bridges. For example, in 1940 the Tacoma Narrows Bridge in the state of Washington, collapsed, after its bridge deck began to wave and twist under the force of a 40 m.p.h. wind. The bridge was only four months old. A 336 foot double-leaf bascule span at Sault Sainte Marie, Michigan, fell, in 1941, while a locomotive was crossing. It had been in service for twenty-six years. On December 15, 1967, the Silver Bridge, that linked Kanauga, Ohio, with Point Pleasant, West Virginia, over the Ohio River, also collapsed, which took the lives of about fifty people.[5]

As the Pacific Railroad expanded westward from St. Louis, Missouri, and reached the capital of Jefferson City, it would suffer its first major railway disaster due to a bridge failure. On November 1, 1855, in a celebration of the line's completion to Jefferson City, the railroad company had invited about 600 souls of St. Louis - citizens, delegates, and several prominent figures, to take an overnight first run trip to the state capital. The 15 car excursion train was pulled by a big twenty-eight ton iron horse locomotive; and while crossing the newly constructed 800 to 900 foot trestle bridge over the rain-swollen Gasconade River, the bridge collapsed plunging ten of its cars 30 feet to the churning river below. Thirty-one or more passengers were killed, including Calvin Case, an associate of James Eads; and about 100 others were seriously injured in the wreckage as well.[6] The St. Louis *Daily Missouri Democrat* reported the breaking headline news in the morning paper, which read: "Terrible Catastrophe! The Excursion Cars to Jefferson City precipitated into the Gasconade River! Probable Death of many of our

Distinguished Citizens!"[7]

Shortly after the Civil War, Eads would begin to dream his dream of a grand bridge over the Mississippi at St. Louis. Learned engineers of his time would deem the daring proposal an impossibility, but one that would become one of the greatest manmade wonders of America. Concerning the man that would soon quiet the skeptics, it was said that "he grappled with great problems in engineering, and solved them as easily as a boy subtracts two from six. While this is true, it must not be forgotten that he had not the school-training of an engineer...He was a very unusually brilliant engineer, and his ignorance of the higher mathematics served to show his brilliancy the more clearly. Some persons have said that his chief talent was in explaining abstruse reasonings simply; but an engineer [once said] that he thought Eads's chief talent was his ability to arrive by some rough means at a certain conclusion to a given problem, which conclusion would in every instance be approximately the same that better trained mathematicians would reach by mathematics."[8]

To the engineering brilliance of James Eads there was no doubt, but for such an undertaking as with his former accomplishments, it would take a great amount of support and finances to bridge the Mississippi. Emerson Gould wrote in his book *Fifty Years on the Mississippi* that, the construction of the St. Louis bridge was a monument "to his public spirit, to his genius, and above all, to his financial ability.

"Whatever credits is due him as an engineer, or for his mechanical and inventive genius, all sink into insignificance when compared to his ability as a *financier*.

"Upon that all his success depended.

"His ability to avail himself of the skill, of the experience and the brains of all with whom he came in contact, was phenomenal and enabled him to succeed in any mechanical proposition suggested.

"The very able assistants and engineers he had employed in building the St. Louis bridge left him very little to do of the detail in construction; but to plan and execute, no man was his equal.

"But only from his transcendent ability as a *financier* would there have been to this day so splendid a structure at St. Louis as the Ead's bridge."[9]

The end result of the Eads' bridge at St. Louis left Walt Whitman impressed, and he wrote about it, saying: "I have haunted the river every night lately, where I could get a look at the bridge by moonlight. It is indeed a structure of perfection and beauty unsurpassable, and I never tire of it."[10]

Before the miracle of a grand bridge over the Mississippi was realized, ferries and steamboats were used to transport freight and passengers from one shore to the other. In the meanwhile, railroads were beginning to pile up on both sides of the river and the need for a bridge at St. Louis was growing by leaps and bounds. James Eads would begin to make his sketches, while his critics scoffed at the impossible notion.

When at last his brave plans were laid bare, despite the power of the river, it showed four massive piers that would be sunk to the bedrock below. The middle foundations further out in the river would span 520 feet apart, while the abutments on each shore would be a connecting span of 502 feet. The arches of steel, never before attempted at this distance, would run gracefully between each pier.

In August of 1867, the equipment and machinery needed to begin bridge construction was being assembled on the west bank. By August 20, work began on the cofferdam at the West Abutment - the dream had begun. Beneath the selected site of the West Abutment were decades of material that would have to be removed. There was a considerable amount of debris from the twenty-nine wrecked steamers of the terrible St. Louis fire of 1849, which included, "old sheet-iron enveloping their furnaces, worn-out grate-bars, old fire-brick, parts of smoke-stacks, stone-coal cinders and clinker, and every manner of things entering into the construction of a

Mississippi steamer seemed to have found a resting-place at this spot...."[11]

The huge piers were all sunk to the bedrock by way of metal caissons which were iron shells formed for underwater construction below groundwater level. The caissons were watertight chambers used to enable workmen to work underwater to remove and excavate a given site. The design of the caissons for the St. Louis bridge were taken in part from some that Eads had seen in France, which he compared to "inverted pans."[12] Open only at the bottom, the airtight work chamber would reach the bedrock with the massive masonry pier being built above. The caisson would sink as the workmen excavated underneath, throwing the sand under pipes leading to the surface to be sucked out. In order to equalize the external pressure due to increasing depth, the caisson had to be filled with compressed air; an opening to the surface; and an airlock to admit passage from one atmosphere to the other. It is an interesting fact that one of Eads' double-turreted ironclads, the *Milwaukee*, which was used by Farragut at Mobile, was purchased, and its thick iron hull used in building the caissons.[13]

One innovation Eads began with his caisson design involved the airlock, which "had always been placed at the top of the entrance shaft, where, as the caisson sank and the shaft was lengthened, it had to be constantly moved up. Eads placed it in the air-chamber of the caisson itself, where it never had to be moved; and thus, as the shaft was not filled with compressed air, less was needed, and there was less danger of leaks."[14] Another change he made was to build the shaft of wood and put a spiral staircase inside it. In the last pier, he went so far as to put an elevator within the shaft. Eads was also the first "to run his pipes for discharging the sand, not through the shaft, but through the masonry itself; and he invented a very simple and effectual new sand-pump, which was worked by natural forces without machinery."[15]

One of the piers reached the depth of about 110 feet, after workmen had removed about ninety feet of gravel and sand from their vantage point under the caisson. They eventually found a smooth rock riverbed worn by eons of time and running water.[16] It was the first time that work of this magnitude, in size and depth, had ever been attempted. In a letter written by Mr. Eads he refers to the deep foundations of the East Abutment which marked a new era in deepwater engineering, saying: "The future is wisely hidden from our view, and I cannot therefore tell what disaster may befall me in sinking the East Abutment pier; but when I left it to-day, I could not help being impressed with the feeling that I had never undertaken any mechanical or engineering performance before with such full assurance that failure was absolutely impossible as in the case of this, the greatest work of my life. Every difficulty that presented itself in the sinking of the two channel piers has been fully provided for in this one, and I cannot believe anything can possibly occur that would prevent my assistants from safely placing the monster mass of masonry exactly where I intend it to rest, even if I were stricken out of existence to-morrow...."[17]

The sinking of the St. Louis foundations, to accommodate the steel arch bridge, also caused a mysterious health hazard for employees of the project - a phenomenon known at the time as the "Grecian Bends." The medical term for the acute disease is called "aeroembolism" and is caused by sudden decrease of atmospheric pressure. Victims of the "caisson disease" experience excruciating pain in many parts of the body and abdomen, as bubbles form in the bloodstream and swelling under the skin, causing workers to double up in pain and walk in a bent over fashion. Modern scuba and deep sea divers simply refer to the sickness as "the bends." As a result, temporary paralysis can occur, and in some cases victims experience permanent damage or even death.[18]

During the construction of the St. Louis bridge "every precaution seen to be necessary was taken; the hours of work were made very short, the elevator was provided, medical attendance and hospital care were given free. After the first disasters no man was allowed to work in the air-chambers without a doctor's permit."[19] Decompression chambers would become the solution to the bends in the future, by placing divers and workmen immediately back into a pressure chamber and slowly returning the pressure back to normal atmospheric conditions.[20] But this procedure would come too late for some of Eads' workers; of the 352 employed to work in the air chambers, 14 perished due to the mysterious air pressure disease.[21]

Out of the souls who suffered and died from the effects of compressed air, there were eight examined *post mortem*. One case which was reported by the coroner, read: "On examining the contents of the cranium, the substance of the brain was found overcharged with blood, oozing freely from minute points on section. The meninges were also highly congested, and considerable serous effusion between them, most marked under the arachnoid. The spinal canal was also opened and examined, and about the same condition existed here as in the brain. The effusion under the dura mater was well marked. There was also found in the inside of the dura mater, at several points, small clots of extravasated blood. In examining the thorax, the small capillaries of the pleura and pericardium were found highly injected. The lungs very highly congested, but much less than the other organs. All the abdominal viscera were entirely congested; clots of extravasated blood were found in the kidneys, and small dark patches on the mucous membrane of the bladder, resembling ecchymosis."[22]

Another *post mortem* examination, said: " The brain and spinal cord were found highly congested, the latter being softened in many places to pulpy consistency. There was evident subarachnoid effusion, and probably more than a normal quantity of fluid in the dura mater of the cord. Small clots of extravasated blood were found at different points on the external surface of the latter membrane. All the abdominal viscera were surcharged with blood, the lungs suffering less in this respect than any of the other organs. There were clots of blood found in both kidneys; one of the ureters was very much enlarged."[23]

There was at least one solution to the hazard tried at the time that was claimed to have been of some aid in overcoming decompression sickness, galvanic bands of metal, that were made of alternate scales of zinc and silver, were worn by the caisson workers. The bands were tried on their wrists, arms, ankles, waists, and even under the soles of their shoes.[24] According to the *Missouri Republican*, March 30, 1870, it reported that "...there has been no workman disabled for a week or so. In fact the fashion of the 'Grecian bend' has almost disappeared from the pier population. There is no doubt but this to be attributed to the voltaic armor now worn by nearly all the men."[25]

In the deepest submarine work of its time that had ever been done, "Eads tells us in his reports many interesting experiments he made in the air chambers. In their dense atmosphere a candle when blown out would at once light again. This was before the days of electric lighting; otherwise we may be sure that that would have been used, as so many other modern inventions were."[26] Other strange occurrences were caused at that depth as well, workman spoke in high pitched tones, and they discovered that they could not whistle in the pressure. Visitors, who dared to venture into the depth of the caissons, found that the odor of workmen, candles and lamps, made for a very unpleasant experience.[27] And for the very first time, "the last pier sunk had telegraphic communications with the offices on shore; which must have been comforting to workmen starting out to their labor in the dead of winter with two weeks' provisions."[28]

The St. Louis bridge was the first bridge not to use spandrel bracing; and the first to use cast steel. The steel arches were constructed from one pier to the other and had to meet in the middle. And for the first time also, put together without "staging from below...All the necessary working platforms and machinery were suspended from temporary towers built on the piers; and thus while the arches were being put-up, navigation below was not interfered with."[29]

With such an enormous undertaking of this size and

scope, as was the bridge at St. Louis, many engineering "firsts" or inventions of necessity had to be produced. One example of this which was caused by an error "of the contractors, presented itself when they came to insert the central tubes to close the arches. The tubes were found to be two and a half inches too long to go in, although they would be only the required length when they were in. Shortening them would of course have lowered the arch. Eads, who was just starting for London on financial business of the bridge, cut the tubes in half, joining them by a plug with a right and left screw. Then he cut off their ends, for the plug would make them any required length by inserting or withdrawing the screws a little...The screw-plug tubes, of course, were easily put in. Any part of this steel work can be at anytime safely removed and replaced, - another structural feature original in this bridge."[30]

There were other obstacles and setbacks that had to be dealt with during the bridge's construction, one such instance was a terrible and deadly twister. On March 8, 1871, an afternoon tornado wreaked havoc on the city of St. Louis and Eads' bridge project. The path of the storm showed a wind force that surpassed anything on record at that time. Lumberyards were swept away; all the framed homes in the path of the funnel cloud were totally dismembered and carried off. Nothing was left where the Belleville Railroad Station had been, but the piles where the building had rested. "Large sycamore trees about three feet in diameter were torn asunder and whole trains of cars were thrown from their tracks. Several empty freight-cars were lifted from the ground and carried hundreds of yards through the air, their trucks falling during the flight and burying themselves in the earth or striking the tracks with such force as to bend the rails completely out of shape."[31]

The frames of the East Abutment were leveled to the water instantly, James Eads explains: "Hydraulic lifting machinery, air pipes and hose, sand and water-pipes, and all the various devices for the rapid prosecution of the work were bent, broken, and carried down by the large timbers of the framework. These latter were mostly 12 inches square and from 50 to 65 feet long, and in falling were broken to atoms. The violence of the storm carried these frames with their top hamper over on to the cabin with which were the air and water pumping machinery and boilers. Copper steam pipes were here bent and twisted and some little damage to the air-pumps was done. Fortunately, the boilers...remained unbroken in spite of the tons of timber and iron suddenly thrown upon the slender roof above them, carrying it down in the general crash upon the engineers and fireman beneath...

"Strange to say in this general ruin, with men almost thick as bees in a hive, but one man was killed and eight wounded, only two of these seriously."[32]

After having drawn out the plans for the two leveled cantilever bridge - worked out every detail - invented equipment used in its construction and patented many - lobbied in Congress - begged for finances - tasked building contractors and overseen firsthand its construction from the top to the depth of the river bottom - May 24, 1874, saw scores of astonished pedestrians strolling on the upper roadway of the Eads bridge treading gracefully across the great Mississippi, unhampered, and heralding in a new age of transcontinental possibilities.[33]

The final spike was driven in by General William Tecumseh Sherman to a 100 gun salute. Furthermore, the bridge was tested on July 1, privately, with the crossing of a trainload of gravel and iron ore. But it was before a huge crowd of onlookers the very next day that the bridge received its final test before the Fourth of July celebration, and a tribute from President U.S. Grant; with other politicians and financiers who planned to attend. Amid enthusiastic shouts of spectators Eads sent fourteen heavy locomotives with their tenders loaded to capacity with coal and water, each with as many a passengers as could hang onto them, back and forth across the bridge's lower roadway testing it on each of the two tracks in different combinations.[34] It was a complete success!

According to James Eads, who had borrowed as many

locomotives as he could to test the bridge, said that he had made it for the weight "of the greatest number of people who could stand on the roadway above, and at the same time have each railroad track below covered from end to end with locomotives, and for this enormous load not to tax the ultimate strength of the Bridge more than one sixth of the strength of the steel of which the arches were constructed."35

Another method of testing the bridge, that was non-scientific, involved the use of an elephant from the local menagerie. It seems that the great beasts are known for their keen, uncanny instinct of sensibility to venturing out on an unstable bridge. As for the Eads bridge, the displaced elephant showed no hesitation in crossing from Missouri to Illinois to the roar of cheering crowds of circus-like spectators who had turned out for a rare chance of viewing the oddity of such an event.

The results of the bridge at St. Louis was said to have "been so useful that while on the one hand the growth of the city was the cause of its being built, on the other it has been one great cause of the continued growth and prosperity of the city. But it had even broader results than that. 'It made a radical change in the conditions of transportation East and West, and it made possible the Memphis bridge and the future New Orleans bridge.'

"And in another direction yet it is peculiarly important. In bridge-building it marks an era, not only because of its strength and beauty and the daring of its design, but also because of its many labor-saving devices, the inventions of a thoroughly practical mind. A distinguished engineer calls it 'a great pioneer in the art of sinking deep foundations and building spans over wide stretches of space, that astonished in its construction the entire civilized world.'"36

Even after many years, his dream that became a reality, marked the genius and bravery of its monumental creation. Only twelve years after it was in service, the Encyclopedia Britannica honored the bridge as "one of the most remarkable structures in the world in character and magnitude."37

Eads never forgot the poor souls who lost their lives in the construction of the bridge, knowing full well the high price that was paid. The inspiring Mississippi, however, would not lose its hold on James Eads, there were other mountains to climb and problems to solve. The incredible achievement of the Eads Bridge did not lose its newly found luster before he had turned his attentions ahead for a solution to yet another future milestone at the mouth of the great river. James Eads would increase overall traffic on the river and open up New Orleans for large ships, by deepening the Gulf bar - making his Mississippi a busy road of commerce.

Chapter 5

Natural Highway To the Sea

The raging current of genius that flowed within James Eads would not subside, it prevailed upon him without rest, much like the Mississippi itself. His single-mindedness, like the Mississippi's rushing current that is ever flowing to the sea, challenged his restless heart. There were other ways he could master "Old Man River" and make it an even greater highway to the sea.

In a presentation given to the Merchants' Exchange of St. Louis to the River and Harbor Convention, James Eads delivered this address, saying: "The improvement of the Mississippi River involves the contemplation of one of the sublimest physical wonders of a beneficent Creator. The boundless reservoirs which supply its channels through such long periods of the year, and make it so valuable to man, and which, if opened simultaneously, would overwhelm the valley and mar its usefulness, are, with that thoughtful care, which orders all things wisely, unlocked in beautiful succession, month after month, by the touch of Spring, as she leaves her home in the tropics to bless the colder regions of the North.

"This giant stream, with its head shrouded in Artic snows, and embracing half a continent in the hundred thousand miles of its curious net-work, and coursing its majestic way to the Southern gulf, through lands so fertile the human ingenuity is overtaxed to harvest their productiveness, has been given by its Immortal Architect into the jealous keeping of this Republic.

"The garden, which it beautifies and enriches, contains seven hundred and sixty-eight million acres of the finest lands on the face of the globe; enough to make more than one hundred and fifty States as large as Massachusetts; acres of the choicest soil in profusion, sufficient to duplicate England twenty-four times over; more territory than the areas of Great Britain, France, Spain, Austria, Prussia, European Turkey and the Italian Peninsula combined.

"If peopled as Belgium and the Netherlands are, and with not half the danger of famine, it would contain four hundred millions of souls - nearly one third of the entire population of the world. Human comprehension cannot grasp the grandeur of such an empire. Human wisdom cannot estimate the wonderful value of such an inheritance.

"This great valley lies between those parallels of latitude that are known to be most conducive to health and to the development of the mental and physical energies of man. In its capacity to produce the cereals, grasses, cotton, sugar, tobacco, hemp, vegetables and fruits of every kind; in the richness and variety of its mineral wealth, the grandeur and value of its forests, its inexhaustible quarries; in a word, in all the natural resources which conspire to increase the wealth and power of a people, the bounty of Providence has been most wonderfully manifested.

"The stream which in every direction penetrates this favored region, and is the grandest natural feature of North America, holds in its embrace the destines of the American people. Sooner or later it must give to the dwellers within this valley, power and dominion over this whole immense continent.

Natural Highway to the Sea   47

"It is the great arterial system of this Republic. Its vital branches and wonderful reticulations permeate and envelop the great body of our country, giving unity to amplitude, value to productiveness, and to the State, resistless power and an existence as enduring as human liberty and intelligence. Through its copious channels, for all time to come, are destined to circulate the sustenance and abundance of its people."[1]

The vast river system of the Mississippi offered much in the way of navigation, but the immense drainage of itself and its tributaries caused serious problems at its mouth. The build up of sediment in the channels left its depth unsuitable for shipping from the gulf, which greatly hampered commerce. Temporary solutions were carried out in the form of dredging, but this proved to be a never ending contest waged over and over again as the depositing forces of the river, the wave forces of the gulf, and mother nature's storms and flooding, continued to be the victor over the ingenuity and persistence of man.

For many years a shipping canal was considered near Fort Saint Philip, "which should be cut through the river bank out to the gulf."[2] There was also recommendations made for the building of jetties, "which by narrowing the channel should deepen it."[3] In 1874 Congress appointed a board to decide on which plan was to be the most feasible of the two. The board "reported in favor of the canal, and against the idea of jetties, which, in its opinion, could hardly be built, could not be maintained, and would be excessively costly."[4]

In a letter written to William Windom, United States Senate, Chairman of Committee on Transportation Routes to the Seaboard, dated March 15, 1874, Eads wrote about river hydraulics and explained in some detail, that: "The improvement of the mouth of the Mississippi proposed by me consists in an artificial extension of the natural banks of one of the passes, from the point where they commence to widen and disappear in the gulf, to the crest of the bar, about five miles distant.

"This method is indicated as the proper one, by the following facts:

"The Mississippi is simply a transporter of solid matter to the sea. This consists chiefly of sand and alluvion, which is held in suspense by the mechanical effect of the current. A small portion, consisting of larger aggregations, such as gravel, boulders, small lumps of clay, and drift-wood, is rolled forward along the bottom. By far the greatest portion is, however, transported in suspension. The amount of this matter, and the size and weight of the particles which the stream is enabled to hold up and carry forward, depend wholly upon the rapidity of the stream, modified however, by its depth. The banks and bottom being chiefly sand and alluvion, are easily disintegrated by the movement of the water, hence the amount of the load lost by any slackening of the current at one place, will be quickly recovered in the first place below where the current is again increased.

"The popular theory advanced in many standard works on hydraulics, to wit, that the erosion of the banks and bottom of streams like the Mississippi is due to the *friction* or *impingement* of the current against them, has served to embarrass the solution of the very simple phenomena presented in the formation of the delta of the Mississippi, because it does not explain why it is, that under certain conditions of the water, it may develop with a gentle current an abrading power, which, under other conditions, a great velocity cannot exert at all. A certain velocity gives to the stream the ability of holding in suspense a proportionate quantity of solid matter, and when it is thus charged it can sustain no more, and hence will carry off no more, and therefore cannot then wear away its bottom or banks, no matter how directly the current may impinge against them.

"In the upper portions of the delta (which, according to some writers, extends a few miles above Cairo [Illinois]), the width of the river is very irregular. When a rise occurs, the current is increased in the narrow parts of the river, and the carrying capacity of the stream consequently becomes greater, and it at once takes up an additional load. When, however, as the stream flows on, it enters a wide expanse, the current is slackened and the excess of load is dropped to the bottom, and thus shoals or bars are formed. From such expansion of channel way, the volume of water, thus relieved of a portion of its load, passes into another one of the narrow parts of the channel, and here its current by contraction is again accelerated, and the increased load which it can carry is immediately scoured up from the bottom and sides of the channel. In the bends, the centrifugal force of the water makes the current more rapid on the concave bank of the stream, and there it usually gets its additional load, and the caving in of the bend testifies to the rapacity of the water at that point of its course. Once loaded, however, it can carry no more, and hence it may sweep around half a score of other bends below with equal velocity, without injury to them. If it encounter another expanse, however, it again loses part of its velocity, and with it part of its load, to be recovered again in the narrow parts of its channel below. It is evident, therefore, that if the channel were at all uniform in size, the current would be more constant, and the alternate depositing and recovery of part of the burden of the stream would be prevented. This loading and unloading is synonymous with caving banks and sand bars.

"The lower part of the river, nearly all the way from Red River to the mouths of the passes, is remarkably uniform in width, and is therefore comparatively free from falling banks and shoals. This part of the river is transporting its load with great regularity, and without interruption, to the sea; whilst that above, owing to the alternating contractions and expansions in its channel, transports its burden with great irregularity, dropping a part here and taking up a part there, and thus by successive stages, from season to season, it is borne forward.

"If the volume of water were constant, it is plain that the river would soon have a current of great regularity; because the deposit dropped in a wide part of the river lessons the capacity of the channel there, by shoaling it, and reestablishes the proper velocity of the current, and thus stops further deposit at that place; whilst at the contracted channel the scour soon enlarges the passage, and consequently reduces the current, and thus further scour ceases at that point.

"In a channel of uniform width, when the river falls, the stream occupies only the narrower parts of it, and if these be still too great to maintain sufficient current to transport the load, the excess is deposited in the channel, which is thus further diminished until the current is thereby accelerated to the proper rapidity, after which it ceases to deposit any more. When the Bonnet Carre crevasse occurred, the river below it (one hundred and seven feet in depth) was shoaled up thirty-one feet, because the volume of water in the river, being lessened by the crevasse, was no longer sufficient to maintain the normal current in a channel large enough to carry the entire river; consequently the current below the crevasse slackened, and the excess of load was dropped in the channel until the bottom was filled up thirty-one feet deep with the deposit. This reduction of the channel was sufficient to reestablish the current and prevent further deposit.

"We see, therefore, that the causes which control the speed of the stream, and those which give to it the ability to hold its burden of solid matter in suspense, are constantly acting in opposition to each other, and thus the equilibrium between them is restored as often as it is disturbed by alternations in volume, or by irregularities in channel.

"We not only learn from this how simple some of the most apparently mysterious phenomena of the river really are, but also how futile it would be to attempt either to enlarge or to diminish the normal size of its channel, anywhere within its alluvial bed. As rapidly as the engineer strives to deepen it without proportionately contracting it, and thus enlarges it beyond the capacity which these natural forces give it, just so rapidly will the current be slackened by the enlargement, and the deposit be dropped there, and thus lessen it again. And as fast as he may contract it, just so fast will the current be increased, and the consequent scour enlarge it again by deepening it. The *magnitude* of the channel is determined by forces which it is neither necessary or profitable for the engineer to encounter. The *form* of the channel he can control and alter. If he widen it, these forces will inevitably shoal it; if he contract it, they will just as certainly deepen it...."[5]

When James Eads made his proposal to Congress in 1874, he said that he would open the mouth of the Mississippi at the Southwest Pass with jetties, and would maintain a channel depth of 28 feet for $10,000,000 at his and his associates own risk. No money "was to be paid by the Government until a depth of 20 feet had been secured when he was to receive $1,000,000, and afterward $1,000,000 for each additional 2 feet, or a total of $5,000,000 was to be paid in annual installments of $500,000 each, conditional on permanence of the channel during the ten years."[6]

Eads' planned jetties were defeated in the House by a large majority in favor of the ship canal, but the Senate did not approve of the canal, instead, another board was selected to make further determinations and on January 13, 1875, the board recommended jetties for - not the Southwest Pass but the South Pass.[7]

Eads was expected to reach a channel depth of 20 feet and at the bottom 200 feet wide, all within thirty months after the act was adopted. He would receive $500,000 for every additional 2 feet depth reached, and likewise with the bottom width until the channel made 30 feet deep and a 350 feet width bottom. He would "receive $500,000, with additional payments, for maintaining the channel. Up to that period the payments of the Government would amount to $4,250,000, with $1,000,000 in addition, earned by Captain Eads, to be retained by the Government for a certain specified length of time as security that the jetties would maintain the channel secured. There was also a provision in the contract which gave Captain Eads $100,000 a year, for twenty years, for maintaining and keeping the jetty works in repair."[8]

Once again Eads was to do the impossible, both in engineering and in business financing. "The terms and conditions upon which he contracted to do the work were so stringent that not another man in America had the financial ability to have raised the means to do the work unless he had been a millionaire himself." Concerning Eads' determination and character over the matter, it was said that: "No man with less ability as a lobbyist, or with less perseverance, or less knowledge of man and legislators, would have ever succeeded in securing the necessary appropriation for doing the work, with nearly the entire government force of engineers opposed to him and his plans."[9]

The opposition to Eads came from all sides, as never before had the Government entrusted so much river and harbor improvement of this magnitude to the private sector. The military engineers who usually handled these matters were opposed to the idea of handing over the project to Eads, and to "permit him to apply a method that had just been condemned in a report signed by six out of seven of the most distinguished army engineers...."[10]

The South Pass, the smaller of the river's three mouths, was not selected by Eads but was nevertheless the choice made by the government commission six to one in favor of the smaller pass. Eads felt that the larger pass would be more adequate for the needs of commerce and a better engineering choice. Even though the smaller pass was selected for the Eads jetties, it was still expected by the Government to reach the depth of thirty feet - the same results as with the Southwest Pass which was Eads' original planned channel.[11]

The terms of the agreement would hold Eads to the responsibility of "keeping the jetties in repair, and for twenty years taking whatever means might be necessary to maintain the thirty-foot channel." The task of maintenance "called for no more than the restoration of jetties damaged by hurricanes, the occasional replacing of wing-dams, gradual extensions at the ends as the bar has advanced, and the continual use of dredges over the bar to preserve the depth beyond the end of the piers."[12]

As to the theory of his jetties and how they would work, Eads, who was also willing to share his knowledge, said that "the amount of sediment which a river can carry is in direct proportion to its velocity. When, for any reason, the current becomes slower at any special place, it drops part of its burden of sediment at that place, and when it becomes faster again it picks up more. Now, one thing that makes a river slower is an increase of its width, because then there is more frictional surface; and contrariwise, one of the things that make it faster is a narrowing of its width. Narrow the Mississippi then, at its mouth, said Eads, and it will remove its soft bottom by picking up the sediment (of which it will then hold much more), and by carrying it out to the gulf, to be lost in deep water and swept away by currents; and thus, he said, you will have your deep channel. In other words, if you give the river some assistance by keeping the current together, it will do all the necessary labor and scour out its own bottom."[13]

Even though many denied that all this was possible and that it would just create other problems at the river's mouth, Eads went to work on his little South Pass. He made his jetties extend from the pass across the bar and into the Gulf; the east jetty ran about two and one-third miles; the west jetty, which stopped opposite of the east one, was about 1 ½ miles long. The west jetty was able to be made shorter because the natural banks on that side of the river extended further out into the Gulf.[14]

The work began in June 1875 when a flotilla of tug-boats, various steamers, launches, a couple of large floating pile drivers, and other assorted craft, made their way toward the South Pass. Soon a base of operations was established that came to be known as "Port Eads," and because of the delta the settlement had to be built on piles driven down deep into solid ground. A few days later the pile drivers began to set two lines of guide-piles which would become jetty borders. These walls, a thousand feet apart, would be about ten feet wide at the top near the shoreline and fifty feet wide out at the end.[15]

The rows of guide-piles would then receive sinking willow mattresses beside them along the riverside. "The mattresses were sunk in tiers, and each tier was weighted well with rock, put in as soon as each mattress was in position."[16] Then upon this foundation of brush mattress and rubble stone, a wall of concrete was built.

While all this was underway the "yellow fever broke out in camp and sent the force scurrying in all directions. Operations were for several months entirely suspended and some of the most valued men on the work were lost through this disease."[17]

The fever first broke out in New Orleans in mid-July 1878. Eads' chief assistant, Elmer Corthell, in his book *A History of the Jetties at the Mouth of the Mississippi* wrote about the sad ordeal, saying: "Every effort was made to prevent its entrance into Port Eads. Every avenue was guarded by rigid quarantine restrictions, which were enforced against pilots, tow-boats, and mail-boats. A case of fever was, however, inadvertently brought to us by one of our own boats, which we were compelled to send to New Orleans for materials and supplies. On August 6th, a few days later, three new cases appeared, and on the next day nine. The indication were that the dreaded disease would sweep through the crowded quarters occupied by the workmen. The conviction that delay would bring sickness and death to this crowd of human beings, far away from sufficient medical help, and that, in any event, the work must stop, led the resident engineer, on the 6th and 7th of August, to discharge the whole force, except a few acclimated persons, and send them away at once, before the place became infected with the disease. Several of those, however, who left at that time were taken sick either in New Orleans or St. Louis, and some of them died. At Port Eads the disease spread, until sixty-four persons, about one-half of the whole population remaining, were taken sick, eleven of whom died...

"This roll of honor, if space permitted, would include

nearly one hundred more, who had been faithful workmen in almost every department, who had been willing and prompt to do any and every hard work, and who had never been found wanting in the hour of need. Some of them covered now by the sands lie in their resting-places near Kipp signal station, keeping watch, as it were, of the work they stood by until death cut them down."[18]

In the process of building the jetties, to help in the scouring, "a big dredge was procured for the bar at the mouth of the Pass, and month after month saw the channel there improve. The most difficult work was that of increasing the height of the jetties by new mattresses, as they sunk beneath the water. Storms often destroyed many of the upper mats, which were not yet concreted."[19]

In February 1876, despite all the problems, the channel at South Pass had already reached thirteen feet deep. By April, Eads, his assistant Elmer Corthell, and most all the inhabitants of Port Eads, were elated to learn that the river's current had deepened the channel to sixteen feet - their labors were paying off - the plan was working.[20]

The channel was made even narrower in 1877, when, "transverse wing-dams were set out from the jetties into the channel, narrowing it to about 650 feet. By December of that year there were 22 feet over the shoals at the head and the bar at the mouth, both channels very broad."[21] The month of July 1879 found "there was nearly 31 feet of water the entire length of the jetty channel, with a twenty-six foot channel 200 feet wide."[22]

On July 8, 1879, government inspector Captain Brown certified to the War Department that the jetties had cleared a 30 feet deep channel from the Mississippi above the Passes all the way to the Gulf of Mexico. It fulfilled the maximum that the law required.[23] The scheme of forcing the river to dredge out its own bottom had worked and everything had come to pass even as Eads had predicted, long before the current had washed away many tons of unwanted sediment to the depth of the sea.

Before the creation of the jetties at the mouth of the Mississippi "only light-draught ships could safely reach New Orleans; but it was so favorite a cotton port many owners would build vessels of unusually light draught, in order that they might make one trip a year to New Orleans with them, although the rest of the time they sailed to deeper ports. As soon as it became known over the shipping world that New Orleans was now open to deep-draught vessels, a great many new ones were built. Thus the Jetties, as much as any other cause, brought in the era of great ships."[24]

It was very fortunate for the nation that James Eads was such a relentless and persuasive soul. "His theories and arguments were sound and logical, his experience of the river was vast; and beyond his aptitude for making technical reasoning simple and clear, his skill as a diplomatist was equal to his ability as an engineer."[25]

High praise was sung in the columns of the New York *Daily Tribune*, March 29, 1879, when a certain reporter commented on the success and popularity of the Jetties after he had sailed along the river front, saying that he had "counted last week no fewer than one hundred and twenty large square-rigged sailing vessels and eighteen ocean steamers. Fully four fifths of these ships come from foreign ports."[26]

The one time engineer who had been deemed an "outsider" in Louisiana, was now heralded in a new light, because the largest ships in the world were now able to sail with their cargo in and out of the South Pass, thanks to James Eads. John L. Mathews wrote in his book *Remaking the Mississippi* concerning the navigable improvements, that: "For all practical purposes New Orleans has had an unrestricted outlet to the sea."[27]

For the selection of the South Pass as opposed to the larger Southwest Pass (which was the more favorable choice of Eads), time soon proved that the overwhelming buildup of traffic over the years showed that the narrow channel was inadequate. It was written in the early 1900's that the "Southwest Pass, which Eads himself had selected as the only proper outlet and on which he had wished to try his hand, is after all to be the real mouth. The $8,000,000 which we have paid to Eads and his estate represents our tuition in jetty building and the premium we have paid on the open channel for thirty years. We might have saved most of it had we followed the sensible old engineer in the first place."[28]

In 1899 Congress authorized a survey to determine the price tag of jetties to be built at the Southwest Pass. Appropriations were received in 1902 for the construction to begin. The contract was to a single firm that built the jetties along the same principles as were the Eads jetties. The foundation mats were 150 feet wide, the north one reached five miles out into the Gulf bar while the south one extended about six miles; they were about 3000 feet apart at the end and maintained a depth of 35 feet. The success of the Southwest Pass was fortunate to have had "the advantage of Eads's experience, and modern science, and the hearty and active cooperation of the government, the contractors have had little or no delay, and have had ample funds."[29]

And so it was that James Eads had answered the call of progress yet again, and further utilized his passion and experience of the Mississippi with the jetties. Elmer Corthell wrote about the future of the parallel dykes, and said that: "In a score of centuries the South Pass jetties may be buried beneath the vast deposits, which the river floods will accumulate upon and even beyond them, as the delta advances into the gulf, and it may be necessary for some generation in the distant future to repeat the work of this; but the *jetty principle* has been so clearly proven to be in perfect harmony with the laws of nature, that either at the mouth of the South Pass, or some pass of the Mississippi River, jetties will be maintained forever. So long as the husbandman tills the soil of the great valley, so long shall he find for his productions a natural highway to the world through an *open river mouth."*

It would be hard to imagine anyone having packed a lifetime with as many as successful projects worthy of fame and fortune as James Eads had done to this point, yet, his genius was not at an end. Knowing that his Mississippi was cut off from the Pacific Ocean there was much yet to accomplish, he must shorten the Pacific shipping route to the Mississippi trade by thousands of miles, by daring to move seafaring vessels overland on a ship railway.

Chapter 6

From Sea to Sea

With all the improvements that James Eads had already made to his Mississippi there was still yet another troubling obstacle that haunted his soul, which if overcome, could wholly open up the great river to world trade. Pacific shipping was forced to travel from the Orient and California around South America and Cape Horn, about 14,000 long miles, in order to reach their destinations of eastern United States and the Gulf of Mexico.[1] There were several ideas being considered dealing with solutions to this costly and timely shipping dilemma - one of course belonged to James Eads.

In the late 1800's Dr. William F. Channing of California had proposed that a ship railroad be built across the isthmus of Tehuantepec, and his idea was published in the San Francisco *Post* 12 March 1882. His concept of the venture was brought to maturity when he "wrote it out in Washington in an elaborate explanatory pamphlet, illustrated it with excellent cuts...and applied to Congress for a charter. He was not able to expend upon it the large sums of money required for the development of the enterprise, and on returning to the city later discovered that it had found a step-father in Capt. Eads."[2]

Another well known diplomat and engineer, Viscount

Ferdinand Marie de Lesseps, a Frenchman, had also joined in the hunt. Having the Suez Canal under his belt, he would eventually become the man to begin to complete the circle of water around the world with the Panama Canal; but he would die in 1894 with legal problems and would not see the project to its finish.

Concerning the Suez Canal, after Ferdinand de Lesseps gained the favor of Egyptian viceroy Said Pasha in 1854, plans to build the Suez Canal to unite the Mediterranean Sea with the Gulf of Suez was underway. The work on the canal by the Universal Company of the Maritime Suez Canal began on April 25, 1859. The 107 mile canal was completed on November 17, 1869, at a cost of $100,000,000, and was opened to navigation that day where the French imperial yacht *Aigle* passed safely through the manmade waterway. Unlike the Panama Canal, the Suez Canal needed no locks, because the Mediterranean Sea and the Gulf of Suez had a compatible water level.[3]

The ship railway that Eads planned to build was to be located at Tehuantepec, which had as an advantage over a canal at Panama about 2,000 miles less to the Mississippi trade. Eads argued that the ship railway would cost less to build than a canal; it could be finished in less time; move ships through at a faster rate; more simply determine its cost and maintain it for less; and finally, it could more easily be expanded to meet the demands of the future.[4]

His first plans for the ship railroad called "for a single track of a dozen parallel rails, and a car with 1,500 wheels. On this car was to be a huge cradle into which any ship might be floated and carefully propped. The car having then been hauled up a very slight incline out of the water, and monster, double-headed locomotives hitched to it, by gentle grades it and the ship were to be drawn across to the other ocean a hundred miles away, where the ship could be floated again. To obviate any chance of straining the ships, all curves were to be avoided by the use of turn-tables."5

As before, Eads received mixed reviews concerning the enterprise, but not to be beaten, Eads "preached this new crusade of science with his customary vigor." He led with his usual abilities of persuasion, with "the soundness of his views, the clearness of his arguments, and the fervor of his wish to benefit his country."6

A debate and controversy arose between ideas and proposals as to Eads' ship railway, Ferdinand de Lesseps' Panama Canal, and the canal being considered at Nicaragua. Eads took his case to Mexico with the hope of gaining their consent for his project. Eads' plan was adapted from simple examples already in common use, and he made his case by saying that science "could do anything, however tremendous, if it had enough money." He was always willing himself to put up his own money, "and he had the most elaborate surveys made, and remarkable models prepared to show the working of the ship-railway."7

Eads was also consulted on a regular basis by various other governments who sought solutions to their own water transportation problems. The reception he received by the Mexican government was favorable, better than that of his own country. He continued to research and fight on for the ship railroad, and in 1880, Eads revealed some of his findings and wrote about them, saying: "I inspected the River Danube for about eight hundred miles of its course, and investigated the cause and extent of the frightful inundation at Szegedin, Hungary, which involved an examination of a hundred and fifty miles of the Theiss River. I also examined the Suez canal to familiarize myself more thoroughly with the question of a canal across the American isthmus, having previously visited the Amsterdam ship-canal and the one at the mouth of the River Rhone. As a member of the Mississippi Improvement Commission I also aided in perfecting plans for the improvement of that river, and the preparation of its report now under consideration before Congress. Within this time I have thrice visited the jetties at the mouth of the Mississippi, besides my visit to the city of Mexico, Tehuantepec and Yucatan..." Eads went on to say that, he had "also at the request of the Mayor of Vicksburg [Mississippi] twice visited that city during the last year to examine its harbor with a view to its improvement."[8]

In January 1887 Eads went to Washington to help push his bill for the project, but because of his failing health, and at the advice of his doctor, he went to Nassau in the Bahama Islands for rest. By February 24 he decided to return to Washington and made reservations on a steamer. Good news arrived informing him that his bill had passed through the Senate, but the old genius, the tired engineer, would never live to learn that his final achievement, the ship railway across the isthmus at Tehuantepec would fail in the House of Representatives.[9]

James Eads died on March 8, 1887, before he had reached the age of sixty-seven. Prior to his death, the energetic, brave and courageous American engineer, told his friends, that: "I shall not die until I accomplish this work, and see with my own eyes great ships pass from ocean to ocean over the land." In a testament to his undying character and zeal of service, he said at last: "I cannot die; I have not finished my work."[10]

Eventually there would be the joining of the Atlantic and Pacific oceans that James Eads had dreamed his dream of, but it would come by way of a canal across the Isthmus of Panama. Through it would travel commercial vessels of all shapes and sizes, and most importantly, the United States Navy Atlantic fleet could reach the Pacific coast and beyond more quickly, and the Pacific fleet could render aid promptly to the Atlantic seaboard in the same way.[11]

In 1880 Ferdinand Marie de Lesseps and his French Panama Canal Company, went bankrupted, after eight years of attempting to make a sea level canal through the isthmus. Then finally in 1905, the Isthmian Canal Commission decided on a lock-type canal through the rugged hills of Panama. The plan was accepted in Congress the next year. In 1907 President Theodore Roosevelt placed the United States Army Corps of Engineers, under Colonel George Washington Goethals, to the task of building the canal.[12]

The 40 mile long canal ran nearly three fifths its length through the Chagres River valley, which became a twenty-two mile long lake by means of the Gatun Dam, that was 105 feet high and 1.5 miles long. The Gatun Lake, about 85 feet above sea level, received three pair of locks which had a lift of about 29 feet; the double locks in the canal enable one ship to be raised while the other is lowered.[13]

The grand opening of the Panama Canal was August 15, 1914, and was considered by some to be one of the greatest engineering feats ever accomplished. Eads' dream of ships passing from ocean to ocean had come to pass, but he would not be there in the flesh to witness it. Had Eads lived to see it, in all probability, it might have just as well happened upon his Tehuantepec ship railway instead of through the canal at Panama.

Being a self-made man as he was, with no formal education, it was said of him by a caring descendent, that: "When he himself was young, he never supposed that he was a genius; but if he had thought this, he would have striven to be the best-read and best-equipped of geniuses; believing that though he might be mistaken about his talent he could make sure of his culture."[14]

Looking back on the eventful life of James Eads, and considering his body of groundbreaking work, the fact of his being a genius is beyond any reasonable doubt. Not only was he unchallenged in mind but he was endowed with great courage and bravery, daring to attempt ideas that many who were more educated considered preposterous. The faith and confidence he possessed in what he considered to be of common sense and good judgment, many times in the face of opposition, enabled him to excel in life and become a model of human inspiration.

Chapter 7

Honored Spirits of Bellefontaine Cemetery

Not far from the river that Eads so loved, in the city where his magnificent bridge joined the east and the west, is the Bellefontaine Cemetery. Located at 4947 West Florissant Avenue, St. Louis, Missouri, the beautiful grounds of this cemetery offers a view into the past of these honorable spirits buried here who sought to participate in the joys of the life and times in which they lived. Its roadways wind and twist throughout its many acres of men and women resting there who helped forge our national heritage. The memorial art within the cemetery reflects in stone our cultural growth.

On March 7, 1849, several prominent citizens of St. Louis organized a group and formed an organization called the "Rural Cemetery Association," procured 138 acres on the Bellefontaine Road (part of the old Hempstead farm), and the movement for a cemetery was underway. Because the cemetery was located on the old military road that led to the site of Fort Bellefontaine, the name was changed from "Rural" to "Bellefontaine" and so became the Bellefontaine Cemetery. The Bellefontaine Cemetery now has about 330 acres of land, 14 miles of road, and over 84,000 interments, with many of them well-known to locals or to people all over the world.[1]

James B. Eads died on March 8, 1887, in the Nassau, Bahama Islands, due to his illness of lung congestion. The St. Louis *Post-Dispatch* March 11, 1887, quoting the New Orleans *Times-Democrat*, said: "The loss, at any time, of such a man would be a calamity to mankind, but at this particular time, in full ripeness of his fame as a great engineer and scientist, when the crowning glory of his long and useful life, that giant work which his genius had conceived and which it was his dearest wish to live long enough to carry forward to triumphal success, needed his master mind, his guiding hand, his death is indeed deplorable."[2]

When news arrived of Eads' death, many could hardly believe their ears. Estil McHenry, who was married to one of Eads' daughters, was quoted as saying: "I asked Mr. Charles Osborne, the agent of the Western Associated Press last night to learn for me where the report had come from. He telegraphed Cincinnati, and they asked William Henry Smith, General Manager in New York. He replied that the information had come by boat to Key West, Fla., from the Associated Press Agent at Nassau, and this morning confirms it in a measure. It will be impossible to learn more definitely until the arrival of the Monticello at Jacksonville on Sunday night or Monday morning, and that boat will in all probability bear Capt. Eads' remains. James F. How will leave for Jacksonville to-night, reaching there Sunday morning, and will accompany Mrs. Eads, Mrs. Hazard and the body back to St. Louis. The funeral will be in St. Louis probably on Wednesday of next week, but nothing can be said positively on that point until Mrs. Eads has been consulted."[3]

The very next day on March 12, more definite information

was received by Mr. McHenry concerning the death and remains of Eads. "A gentleman in Jacksonville, Fla., telegraphed this morning that the remains would arrive at that city Monday morning on the steamer Monticello, accompanied by Mrs. Eads and Mrs. Hazzard. They will come on to St. Louis without delay. The belief expressed in yesterday's POST-DISPATCH that the body would be here Tuesday night or Wednesday morning Mr. McHenry sees no reason to change from today's news. Mr. J.F. How left last night for Jacksonville, Fla., and nothing will be done about the funeral arrangements until Mrs. Eads is consulted. Whether the obsequies will be public or private will depend, of course, upon her wishes."[4]

The shock of Eads' death was felt far and wide, and in the New York *World*, it read: "Capt. Eads was in many respects the most remarkable man that this age has produced. He was self-educated, and in the broadest sense self-made. He was by nature an engineer and his mind seemed adjusted only to grand undertakings. He added millions to the wealth of the country by his restless energy and his massive enterprises. The charge made in some quarters, that there was the taint of the lobbyist about him, was untrue. He sought the endorsement and the aid of the Government in grand and legitimate undertakings because their very grandeur made them worthy of such support. He added luster to the name of America, and, like all great inventors and designers, received far less than he deserved. Commerce will feel for many years the impetus that he gave it, and this generation will doubtless see the realization of his greatest conception - a ship railway."[5]

On the 15th of March a local St. Louis paper reported that Eads' remains would arrive on the 16th over the Louisville & Nashville Railroad.[6] Then on March 17, 1887, James B. Eads was laid to rest at Bellefontaine Cemetery, and attending the funeral that day were many who knew him and mourned his sad loss and passage. The St. Louis *Post-Dispatch* reporting on the funeral, wrote: "The large concourse of old citizens at the funeral, whose gray hairs testified to the length of their friendship, was an eloquent evidence of the place the deceased held in the public esteem. In accordance with the general simplicity that marked the life of the dead, there were no decorations at Christ Church when the ceremony took place. The interior was simplicity itself...."[7]

The St. Louis *Daily Globe-Democrat* also offered its readers news of the funeral of James Eads, and had this to say about it: "The last rites were of the simplest nature, and were performed according to the beautiful ritual of the Episcopal Church. Christ Church was filled with many friends and acquaintances of the deceased before 2 o'clock, and the large concourse testified to the esteem in which he was held by the community. In conformity with the wishes of the deceased and his family, no mourning drapery of any kind marred the symmetry of the interior...."[8]

The choir sang the comforting chant, "Lord, let me know mine end," and Reverend Montgomery Schuyler conducted the order of service for the dead. Schuyler's assistant Rev. Benjamin E. Reed offered prayers, and the 375th hymn was sung beautifully by the choir. While the procession slowly flowed out of the building, the hymn "Lead, Kindly Light" reverberated in the edifice.[9]

When the remains were taken to Bellefontaine Cemetery Rev. Reed read the last words over the dead, "committing to the dust all that was mortal of Capt. Eads."[10] The immediate mourners present were Mrs. Eads, Mrs. Hazzard, Mr. J.T. How, Mr. and Mrs. Estill McHenry, Mr. And Mrs. John A. Dillon, John Ubsdell, Louis How, Dr. and Mrs. C.W. Stevens, Dr. C.D. Stevens, and Ed Switzer.[11]

Also within the confines of the Bellefontaine Cemetery rests General William Clark, who was born in 1770 in Caroline County, Virginia. He was known as a soldier and explorer and became famous with the historic duo - Lewis and Clark. In 1795 during an Indian campaign he met Meriwether Lewis, and by May 14, 1804, the Lewis and Clark Expedition left St. Louis, Mo., into the newly acquired Louisiana Purchase and returned on September 23, 1806. He became a brigadier general and Indian Agent in 1807 for the Missouri Territory at St. Louis. In 1813 Clark became the governor of the territory and dealt with Indian disturbances. He died on September 1, 1838, and was placed in a tomb on his nephew's farm, which is now known as O'Fallon Park. After Bellefontaine Cemetery was established, he was taken and buried there alongside several other family members.[12]

Visitors to Bellefontaine can see the gravesite of Thomas Hart Benton as well. Born near Hillsborough, North Carolina, in 1782, he became Missouri's first Senator in 1821 and served at that position for thirty years. Benton is known for a duel he fought with another prominent St. Louis lawyer, Charles Lucas, which took place on a sandbar in the Mississippi called "Bloody Island" on August 12, 1817. Before he died on April 10, 1858, he had been a successful politician, historian, editor, soldier, and lawyer.[13]

The final resting place of General Sterling Price can also be found at the cemetery. Price was born September 20, 1809, in Prince Edward County, Virginia, and moved to Missouri in 1831 settling near Columbia. He fought in the Mexican War under General Stephen Watts Kearny (who is also buried at Bellefontaine), and became Governor of Missouri in 1852. During the Civil War he led a Confederate cause for Missouri with then Gov. Claiborne Fox Jackson, and became known by his troops as "Old Pap." By the end of the war he had attained the rank of Major General in the Confederate States Army. Price died September 29, 1867, and the funeral procession to Bellefontaine Cemetery was led by a hearse drawn by six black horses. Hundreds turned out, and many of his "boys" as he called them, who had served under his command during the War Between the States, were in attendance.[14]

The beautiful place of burial selected for James B. Eads has left him in good company, and a trip to Bellefontaine Cemetery in St. Louis, Mo., can reveal that this is evident. The grave almost within sight of his passion, the Mississippi River, must leave his restless spirit to wander. Possibly his soul may rise from time to time and comb the streets of his hometown, or it may drift along the waterfront somewhere near the old grand bridge that bears his name. But wherever he may be, you can be sure that the legacy he left us will endure throughout history.

A few other interments at Bellefontaine Cemetery

Edward Bates
Henry Blow
Susan Blow
Adolphus Busch
Frederick Dent
Samuel Hawken
Stephen Kearny
Albert Lambert
James McDonnell
John O'Fallon
Henry Shreve
Sara Teasdale

Chapter 8

In Great American Company

In 1920 James Eads, Daniel Boone, and Samuel Clemens, were honored and elected to the Hall of Fame for Great Americans at the New York University in New York City, New York. Eads became the first engineer to receive such an honor, coming thirty-three years after his death. Four years later, in further honor of his achievements, a ceremony was held there and a bust of his likeness was unveiled.[1] In his company at the ceremony, when Eads was accorded the honor of being added to the Hall of Fame for Great Americans, were two other men who led comparable lives of achievements and were honored.

Daniel Boone, the great American pioneer, frontiersman, trailblazer, Indian fighter, woodsman, rifleman, hunter, trapper and scout, was born in 1734 near Reading, Pennsylvania, to a family of Quakers. By 1753 Boone was living with his family in North Carolina on the Yadkin River, where he traveled into present-day Tennessee and Virginia to hunt and trade furs. When British general Edward Braddock mounted an expedition during the French and Indian War against the French at Fort Duquesne, he served in the forces as a wagoneer.[2]

Boone began to make exploratory trips around the Kentucky River in 1767 attempting to settle that region. Before 1771, Boone, and five other companions, had followed a trail through the Cumberland Gap to eastern Kentucky. Four years later he built a fort and stockade on the Kentucky River on the site of Boonesboro, or Boonsborough. The trail that the old pathfinder established, which led to Boonesboro, became known as the "Wilderness Road." The first Boonesboro wedding occurred the same year of the Declaration of Independence, as the pioneers gathered together by the flickering light of homemade candles made from buffalo tallow and feasted on juicy watermelon celebrating the fruits of their labor.[3]

Boone's life was an eventful one, which earned him the title of being the most famous of the Old Southwest pioneers. In 1778 he was taken and held prisoner by the Shawnee Indians. It was five long months before he was able to escape his captors.[4]

Eventually Boone married Rebecca Bryan and had ten children. One child died as an infant and two were killed by hostile Indians. When the oldest son, James Boone, was taken by a band of Indians and tortured to death, a gang of local settlers set out for revenge. They reportedly even the score by enticing some of the Mingo Indian tribe to drink, and in their drunken stupor the angry deceptive settlers murdered and scalped them. It was even said that one of the Indian women who was with child, was chopped open with a tomahawk and the unborn baby impaled on a stake for display.[5] Barbaric methods such as these must have been used by frightened settlers giving in to fear.

After Boone lost his Kentucky Landholding, because he had failed to file his claims properly, he followed his sons west of the Mississippi settling on land under the authority of Spain. The area he settled in 1799, was in the Ozark region near what is now St. Louis, Missouri; it became United States territory after the Louisiana Purchase of 1803. That same year the 4-story Georgian-style Daniel Boone Home was begun near Defiance, Mo., in the beautiful Femme Osage Valley, and completed in 1810.[6]

For twenty years the Boones' farmed the land and hunted. They spent time combing the Missouri River, and made a path that led to Howard County and the salt licks that are located there. Boone and his sons began to manufacture salt, and the road became known as "Boonslick Trail."[7]

Daniel Boone died in the Daniel Boone Home in 1820, which is now a historic site. It was said that he feared that when he died his bones would be taken back to Kentucky, to the state that he felt had swindled him out of his land. Years later his fears came true and he was officially reburied in the bluegrass state of Kentucky; but many Missourians hold that Kentucky was given a substitute body and the old trailblazer is still at rest in his Ozark homeland.[8] A Daniel Boone Monument is located in Marthasville, Mo., the site selected by Boone for his and his wife Rebecca's final resting place, who was originally buried there.

As for Samuel Langhorne Clemens, better known by the pen name Mark Twain, a name he selected from his steamboat days meaning a "safe depth of water," he was born in Florida, Missouri, November 30, 1835, while Halley's Comet streaked across the sky. He became quite famous and earned his Hall of Fame status with Eads as an American writer and humorist. At the age of four his family moved to the small town of Hannibal, Mo., located on the banks of the Mississippi River where he would absorb much of his inspiration for writing.[9]

In his book *Life on the Mississippi* Twain describes his lazy hometown river port of Hannibal in this way: "After all these years I can picture that old time to myself now, just as it was then: the white town drowsing in the sunshine of a summer's morning; the streets empty, or pretty near so; one or two clerks sitting in front of the Water Street stores, with their splint bottom chairs tilted back against the walls, hats slouched over their faces, asleep - with shingle-shavings enough around to show what broke them down; a sow and a litter of pigs loafing along the sidewalk, doing a good business in watermelon rinds and seeds; two or three lonely little freight piles scattered about the "levee"; a pile of "skids" on the slope of the stone-paved wharf, and the fragrant town drunkard asleep in the shadow of them; two or three wood flats at the head of the wharf, but nobody to listen to the peaceful lapping of the wavelets against them...."[10]

After his father, John Marshall Clemens, a Justice of the Peace, died in 1847, Clemens became an apprentice to a local printer and later he began to write for the Hannibal *Journal*, a paper owned by his older brother. He also served as a journeyman printer in New York City, Philadelphia, and other cities, where he furthered his knowledge of crafting letters. Always drawn to and influenced by the great Mississippi River, he became a steamboat pilot and plied the river until the Civil War made river travel unsafe for the general public. He served briefly in the Confederate army, but decided to abandon that line of occupation after the taste of battle gave him a change of heart.[11]

Clemens then traveled to St. Joseph, Mo., and purchased a stagecoach ticket for $150 to Nevada, which was part of the Utah territory at that time. For eight days and nights Clemens rode the famous overland stage following the Oregon Trail all the way to the Rocky Mountains. The stage traveled through the South Pass, where it then turned south to Salt Lake City and on to Carson City, Nevada, with the entire bone jarring trip taking a total of twenty days.[12] While in the territory he experienced life in the old west and sought his fortune in the mines prospecting for precious metals. Not having much luck at mining, he returned to old familiar ground and became a reporter in 1862 for the Virginia City *Territorial Enterprise*. It was there in 1863 that he first began to sign his published articles using the pseudonym "Mark Twain." His first taste of national acclaim as a writer came when the New York *Saturday Press* ran one of his humorous works of frontier life, which later became his first book *The Celebrated Jumping Frog of Calaveras County and Other Sketches* that was published in 1867.[13]

Before long Twain was traveling abroad and giving lectures to the public. He moved to Hartford, Connecticut, in 1871 after marrying Olivia Langdon where they built an ornate Victorian mansion; he also kept a townhouse off Fifth Avenue in New York City. Falling into the allure of the "Gilded Age" as he called it, he became a victim of several failed schemes to make money. With bankruptcy looming ahead for the Charles L. Webster and Company publishing company, to which he had become a partner, Twain went out on a worldwide lecture tour for the purpose of getting out of debt.[14]

Throughout his writing career Mark Twain penned many books, some have become household names, which include such works, as: *Innocents Abroad* (1869); *Roughing It* (1872); *The Adventures of Tom Sawyer* (1876); *A Tramp Abroad* (1880); *The Prince and the Pauper* (1882); *Life on the Mississippi* (1883); *The Adventures of Huckleberry Finn* (1884); *A Connecticut Yankee in King Arthur's Court* (1889); *The Tragedy of Pudd'nhead* (1894); *Personal Recollections of Joan of Arc by the Sieur Louis de Conte* (1889); *The Man That Corrupted Hadley burg (1899);* among others. The book most now believe to be his best work, *The Adventures of Huckleberry Finn*, was banned in Boston when it was released due to its use of language and content.[15]

On the night of April 21, 1910, as Halley's Comet was once again revisiting the earth as it passed by, Mark Twain, died. He was buried in Elmira, New York, alongside his wife who had died in 1904, and his children who were also buried there. In his old hometown of Hannibal, Mo., at the Mt. Olivet Cemetery rests his father, John Marshall Clemens, his mother

Jane Lampton Clemens, his younger brother Henry Clemens (who died as a result of the explosion of the ill-fated steamboat *Pennsylvania* in 1858), and his other brother Orion and his wife.[16]

These great Americans of the past whose names found their way into the Hall of Fame, are honored citizens who made timeless contributions to their world and the human race. It is to future generations of this that they who give of themselves in this manner should always have a place of honor and remembrance, and among these will no doubt be found the name James Buchanan Eads.

Author's Final Word

As the years go by, and the waters of the Mississippi River flow on to the Gulf of Mexico and into the sea, Eads' work surrounding the river continues to inspire and educate the modern world. It testifies to the character and determination of the man, who with no formal education of his expertise, conceived and executed his daring dreams.

To a nation that for the majority has failed to know James Eads, those who do hold him in high regard. When you gaze out over the river's current, and envision the many miles he walked its dark and murky bottom beneath his diving bell contraption in search of treasure never before recovered to such a degree, you are in awe. If you visit the National Military Park at Vicksburg, Mississippi, and see with your own eyes the Civil War ironclad *Cairo*, one of his machines that was salvaged in the mid-1960's and is on display there, you have to wonder. Travelers to St. Louis' waterfront can't help but notice the Eads Bridge, the first true gateway to the west, one of the cities finest historic landmarks. The many contributions that James Eads saw to completion in his short earthly life gave long-term benefit in his absence.

In conclusion, during the process of researching his life I couldn't help but wonder, what if every soul who ever lived gave as much of themselves as did James Buchanan Eads.

Acknowledgements

I would like to thank my wife Katherine, sons Ryan, Seth (and his wife Rhonda), and Eli, for all of their special contributions during the whole process of making this book.

Thanks to the libraries at the Missouri Universities of Rolla and St. Louis.

My gratitude also goes to the Bellefontaine Cemetery in St. Louis for the time I spent there in reflection. I am also fortunate to have been able to spend time at the St. Louis waterfront admiring the river and the Eads Bridge.

Thanks to all of the authors and publishers for much of the information, the book could not have been possible without it.

Once again, thanks to Laird Towle, Leslie Wolfinger, Corinne Will, Karen Ackermann, and everyone at Heritage Books for further documenting such history.

Thanks to everyone who gave their support.

The Maramec Iron Works near St. James, Missouri, was the site of the first successful ironworks west of the Mississippi River. It was in operation from 1826 to 1876 producing pig iron and wrought iron. It was reported that some of the iron plate that was used in the making of Eads ironclad gunboats of the Civil War came from here. It is now the Maramec Spring Park. The Spring averages about 96,000,000 gallons of water per day.
(Photo by the author)

The Maramec Iron Works. (Photo by the author)

Author's sketch of the USS *Cairo*, one of Eads' city-class gunboats.

A good view of the St. Louis riverfront and the state of Illinois across the wide Mississippi through the Eads Bridge. (Photo by Seth N. Jackson)

The Eads Bridge at St. Louis, Missouri. (Photo by the author)

The East Abutment of the Eads Bridge can be seen across the
Mississippi River. (Photo by the author)

Entrance to the Bellefontaine Cemetery in St. Louis, Missouri.
(Photo by the author)

This marks the spot of James B. Eads' final resting place at the beautiful Bellefontaine Cemetery in St. Louis, Missouri. (Photo by the author)

Emerson Gould was a steamboat captain and an acquaintance of James Eads. He was the author of the book *Fifty Years on the Mississippi: Gould's History of River Navigation* published in 1889. The photo was taken at the Bellefontaine Cemetery, St. Louis, Missouri. (Photo by the author)

The gravesite of Confederate Civil War General Sterling Price at the Bellefontaine Cemetery, St. Louis, Missouri. (Photo by the author)

William Clark at rest in the Bellefontaine Cemetery, St. Louis, Missouri. (Photo by the author)

The gravesite at Bellefontaine Cemetery in St. Louis, Missouri, where Thomas Hart Benton is buried. (Photo by the author)

Chapter Notes

Chapter 1
Eads' Mississippi

1) Funk & Wagnalls New Encyclopedia, Funk & Wagnalls, Inc. 1979; *Missouri: The Heart of the Nation*, by William E. Parrish, Charles T. Jones, Jr., Lawrence O. Christensen, Forum Press, Inc., Arlington Heights, Illinois 1980
2) *Fifty Years on the Mississippi or, Gould's History of River Navigation*, by Emerson W. Gould, Nixon-Jones Printing Company, St. Louis 1889
3) Funk & Wagnalls
4) Parrish, Jones, Christensen
5) *The American Promise: A History of the United States*, by James L. Roark, Michael P. Johnson, Patricia Cline Cohen, Sarah Stage, Alan Lawson, Susan M. Hartmann, Bedford Books, Boston 1998
6) *Missouri: A History*, by Paul C. Nagel, University Press of Kansas 1977
7) *Final Resting Place: The Lives and Deaths of Famous St. Louisans*, by Kevin Amsler, Virginia Publishing Company 1997; *The Story of James B. Eads: Road to the Sea*, by Florence Dorsey, Rinehart & Company, Inc., New York and Toronto 1947
8) Nagel
9) *A Treasury of Mississippi River Folklore*, Edited by B.A. Botkin, Crown Publishers, Inc., New York 1955
10) Dorsey
11) *James B. Eads*, by Louis How, Houghton Mifflin and Company, Boston 1900
12) Ibid.
13) Gould
14) Ibid; Nagel
15) Gould
16) Dorsey
17) Gould
18) Ibid.
19) Dorsey
20) How
21) Ibid.

22) Amsler
23) *Recollections of Foote and the Gun-Boats*, by Captain James B. Eads, Battles and Leaders of the Civil War, Vol. 1, The Century Company 1884-1887
24) *Hardluck Ironclad: The Sinking and Salvage of the Cairo*, by Edwin C. Bearss, Louisiana State University Press, Baton Rouge and London 1966
25) *History of the Navy*, by Rev. C.B. Boynton, Editors addition to *Recollections of Foote and the Gun-Boats*, by Captain James B. Eads, Battles and Leaders of the Civil War, Vol. 1, The Century Company 1884-1887
26) Ibid.
27) How
28) Gould

Chapter 2
The Building of "Pook's Turtles"

1) *The Gulf and Inland Waters: The Navy in the Civil War*, by Alfred T. Mahan, New York 1883
2) *Fifty Years on the Mississippi* or, *Gould's History of River Navigation*, by Emerson W. Gould, Nixon-Jones Printing Company, St. Louis 1889
3) Ibid.
4) Ibid.
5) Ibid.
6) *Thunder Along the Mississippi: The River Battles that Split the Confederacy*, by Jack D. Coombe, Sarpedon Publishers, New York 1996
7) Ibid; *The Story of James B. Eads: Road to the Sea*, by Florence Dorsey, Rinehart & Company, Inc., New York and Toronto 1947
8) *James B. Eads*, by Louis How, Houghton Mifflin and Company, Boston 1900
9) *The American Promise: A History of the United States*, by James L. Roark, Michael P. Johnson, Patricia Cline Cohen, Sarah Stage, Alan Lawson, Susan M. Hartmann, Bedford Books, Boston 1998; Funk & Wagnalls New Encyclopedia, Funk & Wagnalls, Inc. 1997

10) *The First Fight of Iron-clads,* by John Taylor Wood, Battles and Leaders of the Civil War, Vol. 1, The Century Company 1884-1887
11) *In the "Monitor" Turret,* by S. Dana Greene, Battles and Leaders of the Civil War, Vol. 1, The Century Company 1884-1887
12) Ibid.
13) Mahan
14) Ibid.
15) *The Old Iron Road,* by Steven C. Parsons, The Ozarks Mountaineer magazine, Vol. 40, No. 1, 1992; *Maramec Spring Park,* by Phyllis Rossiter, The Ozarks Mountaineer magazine, Vol. 34, No. 6&7, August 1986
16) How
17) Mahan
18) Coombe
19) Mahan
20) *Recollections of Foote and the Gun-Boats,* by Captain James B. Eads, Battles and Leaders of the Civil War, Vol. 1, The Century Company 1884-1887
21) Ibid.
22) *Official Records of the Union and Confederate Navies,* series I, Vol. 22
23) Mahan
24) Eads
25) Ibid; How
26) *Report to the Navy Department on the Eads Steam Turret,* by J.W. King, U.S.N., April 30, 1864
27) *Battle Cry of Freedom: The Civil War Era,* by James M. McPherson, Oxford University Press, New York 1988
28) *The Western Flotilla at Fort Donelson, Island Number 10, Fort Pillow and Memphis,* by Henry Walke, Battles and Leaders of the Civil War, Vol.1, The Century Company 1884-1887

Chapter 3
An Ironclad War

1) *The Gun-Boats At Belmont and Fort Henry,* by Henry Walke, Battles and Leaders of the Civil War, Vol. 1, The Century Company

1884-1887

2) *Thunder Along the Mississippi: The River Battles that Split the Confederacy,* by Jack D. Coombe, Sarpedon Publishers 1996
3) *Official Records of the Union and the Confederate Navies in the War of the Rebellion,* Series II, Vol. 1
4) *The Story of James B. Eads: Road to the Sea,* by Florence Dorsey, Rinehart & Company, Inc., New York and Toronto 1947; *The Gun-Boats At Belmont and Fort Henry,* Walke; Coombe
5) Coombe; Dorsey
6) *The Gun-Boats At Belmont and Fort Henry,* Walke
7) Ibid.
8) Ibid.
9) Ibid.
10) Ibid.
11) Ibid.
12) Coombe
13) *The Western Flotilla at Fort Donelson, Island Number 10, Fort Pillow and Memphis,* by Henry Walke, Battles and Leaders of the Civil War, Vol. 1, The Century Company 1884-1887
14) Ibid.
15) Coombe
16) *The Western Flotilla,* Walke
17) Ibid.
18) Coombe
19) *The Western Flotilla,* Walke
20) Ibid.
21) *The Capture of Fort Donelson,* by Lew Wallace, Battles and Leaders of the Civil War, Vol. 1, The Century Company 1884-1887
22) *The Western Flotilla,* Walke
23) *The Gulf and the Inland Waters: The Navy in the Civil War,* by Alfred T. Mahan, New York 1883
24) Ibid.
25) Ibid.
26) Ibid.
27) *The Western Flotilla,* Walke
28) Ibid.
29) Mahan

30) *The Western Flotilla,* Walke
31) Ibid.
32) *Navel Operations in the Vicksburg Campaign,* by Professor James Russell Soley, Battles and Leaders of the Civil War, Vol. 3, The Century Company 1884-1887
33) Ibid.
34) Ibid.

Chapter 4
Wedding the Nation

1) *Life on the Mississippi,* by Mark Twain, Hartford, American Publishing Company 1883
2) *A History of the St. Louis Bridge,* by Calvin Milton Woodward, Washington University, St. Louis 1881
3) Ibid.
4) Ibid.
5) Funk & Wagnalls New Encyclopedia, Funk & Wagnalls, Inc., New York 1979
6) *Missouri: The Heart of the Nation,* by William E. Parrish, Charles T. Jones, Jr., Lawrence O. Christensen, Forum Press, Inc., Arlington Heights, Illinois 1980; *A Ticket to Tragedy,* by Bill Book, Rural Missouri, Vol. 49, No. 9, September 1996; *Fifty Years on the Mississippi* or, *Gould's History of River Navigation,* by Emerson W. Gould, St. Louis, Nixon-Jones Printing Company 1889
7) St. Louis *Daily Missouri Democrat,* November 2, 1855; as quoted in *A Ticket to Tragedy,* by Bill Book, Rural Missouri, September 1996
8) *James B. Eads,* by Louis How, Houghton Mifflin and Company, Boston 1900
9) Gould
10) *The Complete Writings of Walt Whitman,* Edited by Richard M. Bucke, Vol. 4; *The Complete Prose Works of Walt Whitman,* G.P. Putnam's Sons, New York 1902; as quoted in *Rails Across the Mississippi: A History of the St. Louis Bridge,* by Robert W. Jackson, University of Illinois Press, Urbana and Chicago 2001
11) Woodward

12) How
13) Ibid.
14) Ibid.
15) Ibid.
16) Ibid.
17) Woodward
18) Funk & Wagnalls; Jackson
19) How
20) Funk & Wagnalls
21) How; Woodward; *Road to the Sea: The Story of James B. Eads and the Mississippi River,* by Florence Dorsey, Rinehart & Company, Inc., New York and Toronto 1947
22) Woodward
23) Ibid.
24) Ibid.
25) *Missouri Republican,* March 30, 1870
26) How
27) Jackson
28) How
29) Ibid.
30) Ibid.
31) Woodward
32) Ibid.
33) Dorsey
34) *A History of St. Louis, City and County,* by John Thomas Scharf, Philadelphia 1883; Dorsey
35) Ibid.
36) How
37) *Encyclopedia Britannica* 1886; as quoted in *Road to the Sea,* Dorsey

Chapter 5
Natural Highway to the Sea

1) *A History of the Jetties at the Mouth of the Mississippi,* by Elmer Lawrence Corthell, New York: John Wiley & Sons 1880
2) *James B. Eads,* by Louis How, Houghton Mifflin and Company,

Boston 1900
3) Ibid.
4) Ibid.
5) Corthell
6) *Fifty Years on the Mississippi,* or *Gould's History of River Navigation,* by Emerson W. Gould, St. Louis, Nixon-Jones Printing Company 1889
7) Ibid.
8) Ibid.
9) Ibid.
10) Ibid.
11) Ibid.
12) *Remaking the Mississippi,* by John Lathrop Mathews, Houghton Mifflin Company, Boston and New York, The Riverside Press Cambridge 1909
13) How
14) Gould
15) *Road to the Sea: The Story of James B. Eads and the Mississippi,* by Florence Dorsey, Rinehart & Company, Inc., New York and Toronto 1947; How
16) How
17) Mathews
18) Corthell
19) Ibid.
20) Dorsey
21) Mathews
22) Ibid.
23) Ibid.
24) How
25) Ibid.
26) New York *Daily Tribune,* March 29, 1879
27) Mathews
28) Ibid.
29) Ibid.
30) Corthell

Chapter 6
From Sea to Sea

1) *Road to the Sea: The Story of James B. Eads and the Mississippi*, by Florence Dorsey, Rinehart & Company, Inc., New York and Toronto 1947
2) *Fifty Years on the Mississippi*, or *Gould's History of River Navigation*, by Emerson W. Gould, St. Louis, Nixon-Jones Printing Company 1889
3) Funk & Wagnalls New Encyclopedia, Funk & Wagnalls, Inc., New York 1979
4) *James B. Eads*, by Louis How, Houghton Mifflin and Company, Boston 1900
5) Ibid.
6) Ibid.
7) Ibid.
8) Ibid.
9) Dorsey
10) How
11) *The History of the United States*, by William B. Guitteau, Houghton Mifflin and Company, The Riverside Press Cambridge 1942
12) Funk & Wagnalls
13) Ibid; Guitteau
14) How

Chapter 7
Honored Spirits of
Bellefontaine Cemetery

1) Bellefontaine Cemetery Tour Guide 2003
2) St. Louis *Post-Dispatch*, March 11, 1887; quoting the New Orleans *Times-Democrat*
3) St. Louis *Post-Dispatch*, March 11, 1887
4) St. Louis *Post-Dispatch*, March 12, 1887
5) St. Louis *Post-Dispatch*, March 14, 1887; quoting the New York *World*

6) St. Louis *Post-Dispatch*, March 15, 1887
7) St. Louis *Post-Dispatch*, March 17, 1887
8) St. Louis *Daily Globe-Democrat,* March 18, 1887
9) Ibid.
10) Ibid.
11) St. Louis *Post-Dispatch*, March 17, 1887
12) Funk & Wagnalls New Encyclopedia, Funk & Wagnalls, Inc., New York 1979; Bellefontaine Cemetery Tour Guide 2003
13) *Final Resting Place: The Lives and Deaths of Famous St. Louisans,* by Kevin Amsler, Virginia Publishing Company 1997; Bellefontaine Cemetery Tour Guide 2003
14) Amsler; *Battles and Biographies of Missourians,* by W.L. Webb, Hudson-Kimberly Publishing Company, Kansas City, Missouri 1900

Chapter 8
In Great American
Company

1) *Road to the Sea: The Story of James B. Eads and the Mississippi,* by Florence Dorsey, Rinehart & Company, Inc., New York and Toronto 1947; *Missouri: A History,* by Paul C. Nagel, University Press of Kansas 1977
2) *American Heritage: History of the United States,* by Robert G. Athearn, Fawcett Publications, Inc., New York 1963; Funk & Wagnalls New Encyclopedia, Funk & Wagnalls, Inc., New York 1979
3) *History of Our Country,* by Reuben Post Halleck, American Book Company, New York, Cincinnati, Chicago, Boston, Atlanta 1936; Funk & Wagnalls
4) *The American Journey: A History of the United States,* by David Goldfield, Carl Abbott, Virginia DeJohn Anderson, Jo Ann E. Argersinger, Peter H. Argersinger, William L. Barney, Robert M. Weir, Prentice-Hall, New Jersey 1998; American Heritage
5) *Missouri; Then and Now,* by Perry McCandless, William E. Foley, University of Missouri Press, Columbia and London 1976; The American Journey

6) Athearn; Funk & Wagnalls; McCandless, Foley
7) *Missouri: The Heart of the Nation,* by William E. Parrish, Charles T. Jones, Jr., Lawrence O. Christensen, Forum Press, Inc., Arlington Heights, Illinois 1980
8) McCandless, Foley; Nagel
9) Funk & Wagnalls; *Mark Twain's Hannibal: Guide and Biography,* by John A. Winkler, Becky Thatcher Book Shop, Hannibal, Missouri (Pamphlet)
10) *Life on the Mississippi,* by Mark Twain, Hartford: American Publishing Company 1883
11) Funk & Wagnalls; Winkler
12) Halleck; Funk & Wagnalls
13) Funk & Wagnalls
14) *The American Promise: A History of the United States,* by James L. Roark, Michael P. Johnson, Patricia Cline Cohen, Sarah Stage, Alan Lawson, Susan M. Hartmann, Bedford Books, Boston 1998; Funk & Wagnalls
15) Ibid.
16) Winkler

Bibliography

Amsler, Kevin, *Final Resting Place: The Lives and Deaths of Famous St. Louisans,* Virginia Publishing Company 1997

Athearn, Robert G., *American Heritage: History of the United States,* Fawcett Publications, Inc., New York 1963

Bearss, Edwin C., *Hardluck Ironclad: The Sinking and Salvage of the Cairo,* Louisiana State University Press, Baton Rouge and London 1966

Book, Bill, *A Ticket to Tragedy,* Rural Missouri, Vol. 49, No. 9, September 1996

Botkin, B.A., editor, *A Treasury of Mississippi River Folklore,* Crown Publishers, Inc., New York 1955

Boynton, Rev. C.B., *History of the Navy,* Editors addition to *Recollections of Foote and the Gun-Boats,* by Captain James B. Eads, Battles and Leaders of the Civil War, Vol. 1, The Century Company 1884-1887

Coombe, Jack D., *Thunder Along the Mississippi: The River Battles that Split the Confederacy,* Sarpedon Publishers, New York 1996

Corthell, Elmer Lawrence, *A History of the Jetties at the Mouth of the Mississippi,* New York: John Wiley & Sons 1880

Dorsey, Florence, *The Story of James B. Eads: Road to the Sea,* Rinehart & Company, Inc., New York and Toronto 1947

Eads, James Buchanan, *Recollections of Foote and the Gun-Boats*, Battles and Leaders of the Civil War, Vol. 1, The Century Company 1884-1887

Funk & Wagnalls, Inc., *Funk & Wagnalls New Encyclopedia*, New York 1979

Gould, Emerson W., *Fifty Years on the Mississippi: Gould's History of River Navigation*, Nixon-Jones Printing Company, St. Louis 1889

Greene, Dana S., *In the "Monitor" Turret*, Battles and Leaders of the Civil War, Vol. 1, The Century Company 1884-1887

Guitteau, William B., *The History of the United States*, Houghton Mifflin Company, The Riverside Press Cambridge 1942

Halleck, Reuben Post, *History of Our Country*, American Book Company, New York, Cincinnati, Chicago, Boston, Atlanta 1936

How, Louis, *James B. Eads*, Houghton Mifflin, Boston 1900

Jackson, Robert W., *Rails Across the Mississippi: A History of the St. Louis Bridge*, University of Illinois Press, Urbana and Chicago 2001

Mahan, Alfred T., *The Gulf and the Inland Waters: The Navy in the Civil War*, New York 1883

Mathews, John Lathrop, *Remaking the Mississippi*, Houghton Mifflin Company, Boston and New York, The Riverside Press Cambridge 1909

McPherson, James M., *Battle Cry of Freedom: The Civil War Era*, Oxford University Press, New York 1988

Nagel, Paul C., *Missouri: A History*, University Press of Kansas 1977

Parrish, William E., Jones, Charles T. Jr., Christensen, Lawrence O., *Missouri: The Heart of the Nation*, Forum Press, Inc., Arlington Heights, Illinois 1980

Roark, James L., Johnson, Michael P., Cohen, Patricia, Cline, Stage, Sarah, Lawson, Alan, Hartmann, Susan M., *The American Promise: A History of the United States*, Bedford Books, Boston 1998

Soley, Professor James Russell, *Navel Operations in the Vicksburg Campaign*, Battles and Leaders of the Civil War, Vol. 3, The Century Company 1884-1887

Twain, Mark, *Life on the Mississippi,* Hartford, American Publishing Company 1883

Walke, Henry, *The Western Flotilla at Fort Donelson, Island Number Ten, Fort Pillow and Memphis,* Battles and Leaders of the Civil War, Vol. 1, The Century Company 1884-1887; *The Gun-Boats At Belmont and Fort Henry,* Battles and Leaders of the Civil War, Vol. 1, The Century Company 1884-1887

Wallace, Lew, *The Capture of Fort Donelson,* Battles and Leaders of the Civil War, Vol. 1, The Century Company 1884-1887

Webb, W.L., *Battles and Biographies of Missourians,* Hudson-Kimberly Publishing Company, Kansas City, Missouri 1900

Winkler, John A., *Mark Twain's Hannibal: Guide and Biography,* (Pamphlet), Becky Thatcher Book Shop, Hannibal, Missouri

Wood, John Taylor, *The First Fight of Iron-clads,* Battles and Leaders of the Civil War, Vol. 1, The Century Company 1884-1887

Woodward, Calvin Milton, *A History of the St. Louis Bridge,* Washington University, St. Louis 1881

Newspapers, etc.

Bellefontaine Cemetery Tour Guide 2003
Missouri Republican, March 30, 1870
New York *Daily Tribune,* March 29, 1887
St. Louis *Daily Missouri Democrat,* November 2, 1855
St. Louis *Daily Globe-Democrat,* March 18, 1887
St. Louis *Post-Dispatch,* March 11, 1887
St. Louis *Post-Dispatch,* March 12, 1887
St. Louis *Post-Dispatch,* March 14, 1887
St. Louis *Post-Dispatch,* March 15, 1887
St. Louis *Post-Dispatch,* March 17, 1887
St. Louis *Post-Dispatch,* March 11, 1887, quoted the New Orleans *Times-Democrat*
St. Louis *Post-Dispatch,* March 14, 1887, quoted the New York *World*

Chronology

May 23, 1820--James Buchanan Eads was born in Lawrenceburg, Indiana, to Thomas and Ann Eads. Colonel Thomas Clark Eads was a descendent of a substantial family from the state of Maryland.

September 6, 1833--James Eads and his family arrive in the St. Louis area as their steamboat is engulfed in flames.

March 1839--James Eads becomes a purser's clerk (mud clerk), on the steamboat *Knickerbocker*. The boat sinks after being ripped open by a snag a few months later.

1842--Eads joins with Nelson & Case and builds the submarine No. 1 for underwater salvage.

1848--Submarine No. 2

1849--Submarine No. 3

May 17, 1849--Great St. Louis fire.

1851--Submarine No. 4

1857--There were 12 submarines by this time.

April 12, 1861--Shots fired on Fort Sumter. The Civil War begins.

August 7, 1861--Eads signs contracts to build seven ironclad gunboats.

February 6, 1862--Eads' ironclads capture Fort Henry.

March 9, 1862--Historic battle of the *Monitor* and the *Merrimac*.

February 25, 1868--Eads' St. Louis bridge cornerstone-laying ceremony was held.

March 8, 1871--A deadly tornado hits St. Louis.

July 4, 1874--St. Louis celebrates the completion of the Eads Bridge over the Mississippi River.

June 12, 1875--Work began on "Port Eads" at the gulf inlet.

October 5, 1876--The channel at South Pass had reached 20 feet in depth due to Eads' jetties.

July 10, 1879--The South Pass channel makes a depth of 30 feet.

February 24, 1887--Eads receives news informing him that his bill for his planned ship railway across the Mexican Isthmus of Tehuantepec had passed in the Senate.

March 8, 1887--James B. Eads dies before the age of 67.

August 15, 1914--The Panama Canal opens.

1920--Eads was elected to the Hall of Fame for Great Americans at New York University along with Samuel Clemens (Mark Twain) and Daniel Boone.

Index

A

Adam & Noah 1
Aigle 60
Algonquin (Indians) 1

B

Bates, Attorney-General 6
Beauregard, Pierre G.T. 26
Bellefontaine Cemetery 65, 66, 67, 68, 69, 79
Benton 14, 15, 27
Benton, Thomas Hart 69
Bonnet Carre 50
Bonne, Daniel 3, 71, 72, 73
Bloody Island 69
Braddock, Edward 72
Brown, Captain 55
Buchanan, James 3

C

Cairo 11, 12, 48, 77
Cairo, Illinois 4, 6, 7, 26
Charleston, North Carolina 6, 20
Carondelet 11
Carondelet 11, 12, 16, 21, 23, 24, 26, 27, 28,
Carson City, Nevada 74
Case, Calvin 33
Chickasaw 15

Chickasaw (Indians) 2
Cincinnati 11, 12, 21
Clark, William 68
Clemens, Henry 76
Clemens, Jane Lampton 76
Clemens, John Marshall 74, 75
Clemens, Samuel 3, 71, 73
Columbus, Kentucky 26
Commerce, Missouri 26
Conestoga 21, 29
Corthell, Elmer 54, 57

D

Defiance, Missouri 73
DeKalb 12
Demologus 9
Dover, Tennessee 26
Dunnington, Lieutenant 29

E

Eads 3, 4, 5, 6, 7, 9, 11, 12, 13, 14, 15, 17, 19, 23, 24, 29, 31, 32, 34, 35, 36, 37, 38, 39, 40, 41, 42, 43, 45, 47, 51, 52, 53, 55, 56, 57, 58, 59, 60, 61, 62, 65, 66, 67, 68, 69, 71, 76, 77, 78
East Abutment 37, 40
Ellet, Charles 31
Elmira, New York 75

Encyclopedia Britannica 42
Essex 21

F

Fitch, Graham N. 29
Foote, Flag Officer 15, 19, 20, 22, 24, 27, 28
Fort Bellefontaine 66
Fort Donelson 22, 23, 24, 25, 26
Fort Duquesne 72
Fort Henry 19, 21, 22
Fort Saint Philip 47
Fort Sumter 6
Fremont, General 14
Fry, Joseph 29
Fulton, Robert 9
Fulton the First 9, 10

G

Galena, Illinois 5
Garden City 5
Gasconade River 33
Gatun Lake 63
Goethals, George Washington 63
Gould, Emerson W. 2, 3, 34
Grant, General 23, 26, 41
Greene, Dana S. 12
Gwin, William 21

H

Hannibal, Missouri 31, 73
Hartford, Connecticut 75

Hindman, Thomas C. 29
Housatonic 20
How, J.F. 67
How, Louis 4, 68
Hunley, H.L. 20

I

Island Number Ten 23, 26, 27

J

Jackson, Claiborne Fox 69
Jack Tars 16

K

Kanauga, Ohio 33
Kearny, Stephen Watts 69
Keokuk, Iowa 4
Kickapoo 15
King, J.W. 15
Kipp (signal station) 55
Knickerbocker 3

L

Langdon, Olivia 75
Lawrenceburg, Indiana 3
Lesseps, Viscount Ferdinand Marie de 60, 61, 62
Lewis, Meriwether 68
Lexington 21, 29
Louisville 11, 12, 24

M

Mahan, Alfred T. 9

Maramec Iron Works 13
Maramec Springs, Missouri 13
Marthasville, Missouri 73
Mathews, John L. 56
McHenry, Estil 66, 67, 68
Meigs, Quartermaster General 7
Merrimac 11, 12, 15
Milwaukee 15, 36
Mingo (Indians) 72
Monitor 11, 12, 15
Mobile, Alabama 20
Mound City 11, 12, 29
Mound City, Illinois 11
Mt. Olivet Cemetery 75

N

Nassau, Bahama Islands 66
Nelson & Case 4
Neptune 6
New Madrid, Missouri 26, 28
New Orleans, Louisiana 2
New York City, New York 9, 71

O

O'Fallon Park 69
Ojibbeway (Indians) 2

P

Paducah, Kentucky 5
Panamal Canal 60, 61, 62, 63
Pennsylvania 76
Phelps, S.L. 21
Pittsburg 11, 12, 24, 26, 28

Pittsburg, Pennsylvania 13
Point Pleasant, West Virginia 33
Pook's Turtles 17
Pope, General John 26, 27
Port Eads 53, 54, 55
Porter, Captain David 10
Porter, W.D. 21
Price, Sterling 69

R

Roman Catholic 26
Roosevelt, Theodore 63

S

Sainte Marie, Michigan 33
Schuyler, Rev. Montgomery 68
Sherman, William Tecumseh 41
Shiloh, (Battle of) 28
Shirk, J.W. 21
Smith, William Henry 66
South Pass 51, 52, 53, 55, 56, 57
Southwest Pass 56, 57
Spaulding, L. 21
St. Charles, Arkansas 29
Stemble, R.N. 21
Stevens, C.W. 68
Stevens, Dr. C.D. 68
St. Joseph, Missouri 74
St. Louis 11, 12, 21, 24, 29
St. Louis, Missouri 11, 33, 65, 68, 69, 70, 77

Submarine No. 7 11, 13
Suez Canal 60
Switzer, Ed 68

T

Tacoma Narrows Bridge 33
Tehuantepec 59
Tilghman, General 22
Tomb, James H. 20
Twain, Mark 2, 31, 73, 75
Tyler 21

V

Vicksburg, Mississippi 29, 62, 77
Virginia 11

W

Walke, Henry 16, 21, 22, 23, 24, 27
Webster, Charles L. 75
White Cloud 5
Windom, William 47
Winnebago 15
Woodward, Calvin Milton 32

www.ingramcontent.com/pod-product-compliance
Lightning Source LLC
Chambersburg PA
CBHW070505100426
42743CB00010B/1769